Transformation 2020

A Ladies' Power Lunch Anthology

Elizabeth B. Hill, MSW & Dr. Davia H. Shepherd

with Jacqueline A. Baldwin, Julia Bernadsky, Kacey Cardin, Robin H. Clare, Kristina Crooks, Maryann Cruz, Dee DiFatta, Lisa Braidwood Ferry, Robin Finney, Lynn Gallant, Angel Johnstone, Gina Marecki, Donna Martire Miller, Melissa Molinero, Lori Raggio, Mary Roy, Candi Sterling, Kristi H. Sullivan, and Noelymari Sanchez Velez

Green Heart Living

Transformation 2020
A Ladies' Power Lunch Anthology

ISBN (paperback): 978-0-9991976-7-7
ISBN (ebook): 978-0-9991976-6-0

Cover design by Elizabeth B. Hill & Teresa Hnat

Dedication

For future butterflies, in the cocoon.

What if you are in exactly the right place,
at exactly the right time?

What if you are just where you are supposed to be?

What if everything you've put in, is just about to pay off?

We've been there.

We've got you.

Kayla—
Thank you for all your support, for your friendship and how you
Dador Taino helped me in my journey. It will always be Home to me.

much love
herman zuc—

♥ xoxoxo

12/2020

Acknowledgments

First off, I would like to acknowledge all the authors who have been bold and courageous enough to share their stories here on these pages. I am so very proud of you.

Immense gratitude goes to Audra Garling Mika for her editorial and emotional support. Audra went above and beyond.

Thank you to Jaime Williams of Coordinated Creativity Virtual Solutions for her guidance, administrative support, and dear friendship. It appears the strategic planning is paying off.

Jim Williams - thank you for your masterful creation of the Green Heart Living podcasts and for being my dear friend.

I would like to thank my friends and co-creators in Ladies' Power Lunch, e-Women Network, and the Writers' Hive. Who knew work could be so fun?

I would especially like to thank my business coach, Gina Raposa Johnson, my life coach, Kathleen Troy, my organizational coach, Benjamin Albert, and my self-care guru, Kristi Sullivan. Your guidance and care have made more possible than I ever imagined.

I've saved the best for last. My children, Raven and James. Thank you for going with the flow for another publishing endeavor. Thank you for doing heavy lifting beyond your years. Thank you for being creative, loving, funny, intelligent folk. Thank you for making the matriarchal palace more delightful each day. You are amazing humans. I love you bunches.

Table of Contents

Dear Reader,

Transformation can feel very lonely. There are times in a transformation where we must go inward. Sometimes we must curl up in the mess of it.

Here in these pages, 20 authors share inspiration and the experiences that transformed their lives. Some of the stories are intense. Sometimes it's ewwy-gooey in the cocoon.

There is heartbreak, confusion, pain, guilt, anger, and fear.

There is light, hope, passion, peace, purpose, comfort, wisdom, and love.

Most important, there is a way forward.

When you read, I invite you to get as cozy as you can and be in a space to witness these stories. Let the reading be a transformative process in and of itself.

Our authors are courageous. Hold them in your hearts. And when you see yourself in them, know that you are not alone.

Love & Courage,

Elizabeth

Foreword

Dr. Davia H. Shepherd

I watched the billowing black smoke coming from my engine. The lights on the dashboard flickered and came on, even the ones I had no idea were there. Then the dashboard went dark. No more sounds came from the engine, and my headlights were gone. I felt for brakes and sighed in absolute relief as I felt their reassuring tug. I quickly surveyed my environment. A winding road headed downhill, the woods on my right, and a steep ravine on my left.

I have a routine gratitude practice and it suddenly dawned on me that I had never written in my gratitude journal about being grateful for brakes. Hand sanitizer and Lysol wipes, yes, but not brakes, never brakes. Though they had never been my object of affection, here they were, still working when it seemed everything else in my car had stopped. Here they were bringing me to a complete stop. My relief was palpable.

The evening started out just like any other Friday evening. It was late summer 2020 when the evenings had started to get darker just a little earlier. I left work, hopped into my car, and, sort of on auto-pilot, started making my way home. On my drive through back roads to avoid dreaded traffic, my only thoughts were: dinner, shower, rest – maybe not in that order. I had no idea that I'd be starring in my own personal action movie in just a few minutes.

I was jerked out of my idyll by the smell of something

burning. I was so close to home at this point, probably less than a five-minute drive. I looked around to see if any other cars were passing. After all, my windows and sunroof were down, allowing me to enjoy the cool evening. Since there were no other cars, the burning was probably from my car. That's when I saw the smoke. Surprisingly, that moment is also when I felt an overwhelming sense of calm and knew immediately that everything was going to be alright.

I had so many opportunities for panic. But the in-the-nick-of-time escape from the explosion like we see in *The Fast and Furious* never happened. Headed downhill and on a corner at the time of the fire, I had a momentary thought about being parked in the dark on a lonely rural road where people usually speed around those corners. I had no working flashers, but that sense of calm prevailed and I knew all was well. I checked my phone to call for help: thank goodness I had service in this usually-dead zone, but my cell phone battery was quickly dying, and my husband was not picking up my call.

If I had had this same experience just a few short years ago I'm not sure my reaction would have been the same. Panic may have ensued and we all know that panic is the enemy of rational thought. This was an opportunity for me to see in action that the things I teach do help life go better for everyone...even me. My daily practice pays off big.

As I called my husband for the sixth time (I knew I wouldn't have enough cell battery to have a conversation with the tow company's automated system), I remembered my mentor's words for every tough situation: "I am positively expecting GREAT results, no matter what I see in front of me." I took a deep breath, relaxed, and at that moment my husband picked up.

Another thing I don't remember including in my gratitude

journal before now: Cell phones and a cell phone battery with just enough charge when you need it the most.

The story has a happy and anticlimactic ending. My husband called the towing company and they arrived in less than an hour. He found child care quickly for our children who were with him at home at the time and rushed to my rescue. He parked behind my car on that precarious mountain with his flashers on to warn oncoming traffic. He brought me a portable cell phone battery charger. (Yet another thing to add to my list of things to remember to be grateful for.)

I am grateful for this experience because it has given me an opportunity to observe my processes in action and to see that they do have tremendous value.

Let me tell you how I got here, to this place of calm, and stop me if you have heard this one before: We've all heard the quote, "Out of the most challenging times come the greatest transformations." I was no different, y'all. If you'd met me 10 years ago you'd have met a truly different person on many levels. For one: I was in excruciating pain. The irony of this is not lost on me; I am a doctor who treats mostly patients with headache, neck pain, and back pain, yet, I was in the office treating patients while I was on crutches. In a way I was a victim to the "toxic sense of self sufficiency," that our society embraces. I'd seen six different doctors and endured one unnecessary surgery with no results. That's when one of my patients, who I now know was the voice of Source, said to me: "Doc, you need to go take care of yourself."

For the first time in the history of my world, I, the overachiever who usually would be in the office six days a week to see patients no matter the weather, closed my office for the first time ever to take care of me. The truth is, things were bad. I was

NOT WELL! And, the bigger truth is: things didn't have to get to that stage. Or maybe it had to for me to get my wake-up call?

I had given myself none of the grace I ALWAYS give to others. I had burned myself out and now had an unwanted long-term diagnosis. I used the functional medicine tools that I typically give to my patients and helped myself. Out of that whole kerfuffle was born a new way of living my life that not only improved my health, but also expanded my business.

I had gotten into the habit of doing things myself, always. Being an over-worker, or workaholic, had become a part of my identity. In order for me to truly heal, I needed to let go of that. This is something I work on every day.

I needed to learn how to receive help, how to delegate without fear. I had to learn the power of having a strong supportive community, and how much more fun and easier life is within the warm embrace of a collective. I know I'm mixing my stories here, but I'm talking about supportive communities like emergency caregivers, like having someone who will come get me off the side of a mountain if need be. And one more thing I had to remember, or rediscover, is that I am always supported by Source.

Here are the five steps that have supported me from burnout to brilliance. I call them my five P's! These are steps that I work through with patients and clients. They are simple little tweaks that have been life changing for me.

1) *The Pictures*

In the past, I felt emotions based on what was showing up in my life, the pictures of my life, if you will. If things were great and the sun was shining, then I'd have a big smile, and if things were going to the dogs, then my mood would be too. This groundbreaking idea of not letting the circumstances of your life be the reason you feel the way you feel just seemed crazy to me, but working with multiple coaches, reading numerous books by guru after guru saying the same thing encouraged me to at least give it a 30-day money-back trial. That was many 30 days ago. Granted, there have been ups and downs on this journey and everyday is a new day with this. What I know now is that we don't need for the pictures of our lives to look perfect in order to feel inner peace and joy. I now can embrace that I don't need great circumstances to feel good. I truly believe in the support of the universe. And as my dear friend, Aina, says, "I live my life from the inside out."

2) Practice

I'm still a work in progress every single day. Growing up, I didn't learn this way of being. What I learned and what was modeled to me was: There are some things that are just beyond your control. What I know now is I always have control over my emotions and how I choose to feel in any given situation. That doesn't mean that unpleasant things don't happen at all or that I look at the world through rose-colored glasses. I mean, were you here for the part of the story when I was sliding down a steep, treacherous mountain road in a car on fire? What it means is that because I am practicing every day to maintain my inner peace, on the days when I need it most I'll be better able to weather the storm. I actually practice feeling good more of the time. It's like a muscle; I build it with use.

3) Processes

To practice feeling good more of the time, my recommendation is to develop your daily routine to include:

meditation, gratitude, affirmations, and journaling.

a) Morning Routine

There is a little space in the morning when I wake up, when I know I'm awake but before I start planning my day and going off on all my tangents. I try my best to get control of my thoughts in this space and consciously project thoughts of appreciation and gratitude. Appreciation for another day, for health, for my family, for my internal plumbing working the way it should as I rush off to the bathroom.

Once I'm squared away, I try to introduce some movement or exercise. Yoga works well for me, and then I spend a few minutes meditating. I do a spot of journaling, and then I listen to or read something inspirational to help set the tone for my day.

This means for me that I have to get up a bit earlier so as not to be disturbed by my little ones, but the time is worth it, and I notice that on the days that I miss incorporating this routine, it is a little harder to navigate challenges. I also avoid all media, social and otherwise, during this time. The emails will still be there when I'm done!

b) Daily Routine

One of my mentors is a teacher of universal law. She introduced me to deciding how I want to feel before I move into each different portion of my day. As I am walking into the kitchen to prepare breakfast for my kids, for example, I remind myself that I want to feel efficient and in flow; as I drive to work, I tell myself I want to feel safe and secure; as I go through the day treating patients, I intentionally focus on wanting to feel in flow and knowledgeable; when I return home to my family I want to feel love and joy...and patience; going to bed I want to feel relaxed and in gratitude.

You can break this down into even smaller chunks of time, but what this ensures is that you are at all times paying attention to how you feel. And then the kicker for this is to ask yourself after each segment: How did I feel during this segment? I find this builds more awareness into each day.

c) Don't Beat Yourself Up

There are days when my morning "glow" lasts longer than others. On some days I'm rushing so much that I'm not paying attention to how I want to feel and wander into uncomfortable emotional territory. On some days, things just overwhelm me. That's OK.

Let's promise to not beat ourselves up for not being happy enough! Every day we have an opportunity to continue our practice and every day our happiness muscle builds and gets stronger, helping us handle the toughest situations with ease, detachment, calm, peace, and grace.

4) Personal Care

We've all heard that you can't pour from an empty cup and that you should put your oxygen mask on first before helping others. These are not just platitudes. Sometimes, no matter how hard we try to reach for happiness, it may elude us because of something physiological.

Have you ever noticed that when you feel healthier, well-rested, well-hydrated, when you are fed, when you have exercised, and when you have avoided negative people, places and things, that you feel amazing, like you could conquer the world? Let me put on my physician and recovering researcher hat here for a minute to say, yes, there is a change in your brain and body chemistry in response to all these things. As women, we tend to take care of everyone. Let's be sure to take care of our health, too!

Are you taking care of your food and nutrients, hydration, sleep, exercise, brain breaks? Are you avoiding negativity? Will you seek professional help when necessary?

5) People

Seven years and change ago, six women got together in a Ruby Tuesday on Route Six in Bristol, Connecticut. They were friends who tried so hard to make time to see each other, but found it difficult with family and work obligations. Finally, they arrived at a date and time that worked for everyone and they met and enjoyed an amazing lunch. I was one of those women.

It was a day I'll never forget. It seemed as though time stood still in a magical moment. Everyone around that table was there to support the others. Anyone who had a question found someone in the group who could answer or point in the direction of a solution. I was at that stage in life where I had just gone through a terrible health ordeal, my baby was still small, and my practice was experiencing growing pains. Everyone at the table could relate, be a listening ear, give some advice, make a connection. It was that way for all of us. We all benefited tremendously from making that time to be together. It dawned on me in that moment the power that is available to us when we get together. Suddenly it's not just 1+1=2; the results are exponential.

As we hugged each other (back when hugging was a thing), wishing we could spend more time, someone suggested a brilliant idea: Why don't we do this much more often? Out of that amazing day a movement was born. Ladies' Power Lunch is a group of women in business who intentionally and regularly support each other. I invite you to join us at ladiespowerlunch.com.

I'm not sending you to go start your own movement unless you truly want to, but I am suggesting being part of an outstanding community. Let go of the idea of having to do it all on your own. Embrace that everything is easier with a collective of like-minded, supportive individuals. Understand that success is so much more likely when we can ask the audience or phone a friend. Let's look for opportunities for heart and soul connecting.

Selah.

About Davia

Dr. Davia H. Shepherd is a holistic physician and master connector. A certified retreat leader and recovering researcher, she is celebrating almost 20 years in various areas of healthcare. She loves public speaking and is an international speaker and bestselling author. She helps female entrepreneurs live the best version of their lives in every area: health, business, relationships, finances. She leads transformational retreats, conferences, and free monthly Ladies' Power Lunch events. Davia lives in the suburbs in Connecticut with her outstanding husband, Wayne, two amazing miracle boys, Preston and Christian, and her mom, Phyllis.

"Because I'm practicing every day to maintain my inner peace, on the days when I need it most I'll be better able to weather the storm."

Dr. Davia H. Shepherd

power-transformations.com

Love

forgiveness
acceptance
wholeness
light
ignited

Chapter 1

Letter of Forgiveness

Dee DiFatta

Dear Little Dee,

I forgive you for living by default instead of by design. Up until this year, you have allowed other people and circumstances to define you and deter you from living your deepest desires. It has taken 48 years of life, 26 years with multiple sclerosis, and 17 years working full-time in insurance, to realize that your limited reality is not your truth.

On February 14, 2020, you were brave enough to listen to your intuition and take an incredible leap of faith. You resigned from your full-time job in order to pursue your purpose and passion as a motivational speaker, educator, and author.

Who knew that by finding the courage to end this chapter of your life it would open a portal to so many new beginnings? Two weeks after resigning, the heavens opened and sent you a gift. A life coach appeared on Facebook and asked, "What do you want out of life? And why do you want it? It's time to set some intentions and learn to live life from your higher self."

These words empowered you into action. And you stepped up, stepped outside of your comfort zone, and made an appointment with this life coach.

On March 15, 2020, you reached a pivotal crossroad.

Coronavirus was starting to shut down the world. And you were forced to choose between living from fear and worry or living from faith. You had to dig deep for the inner strength necessary to keep the appointment with the life coach, but you did it. And in that one seemingly insignificant moment, you said, "Yes" to you, "Yes" to your life coach, and "Yes" to God. You chose inner calm over outer chaos.

Up until this life-changing moment, you had been afraid to face your fears and live your truth. You had been living life from limiting beliefs and perceptions that you inherited growing up. And these illusions caused a lot of confusion. For 48 years, you had been trying to find love, acceptance, and validation from others but, in doing so, you lost a part of yourself. And now was the time to stop the madness within. You were not meant to live in survival mode. You were born to thrive.

In order to be truly aligned with the new design you have created for yourself, it's time to start down the freedom trail of forgiveness. By going within and forgiving yourself, you set yourself free to just be. No more expectations. No more judgments. It's time to release the guilt, resentment, blame, and shame. These emotions are no longer serving you. It's time to be the inspiration you were born to be.

I forgive you for trying to hold on and stay in control during this pandemic. You were under the impression you had to be strong for your family and your followers. But that is an old limiting belief you have been carrying with you through life. You are not responsible for everyone else. God is there for them the same way he is always here for you. Let this misperception go and allow your blessings to flow.

I forgive you for always trying to be positive. Not every day is going to be a good day, and sometimes you need to embrace the darkness within to truly find the light. When you keep avoiding the darkness, you don't escape it. It's time to take responsibility for the good, the bad, the ugly. Choose to sit in the darkness and find the lesson and the blessing in it. By embracing the dark, you take its power away. And you continue to get stronger every day.

I forgive you for not sharing your feelings and emotions. Up until now, you were afraid to let go and let your tears flow. You held onto the illusion that this made you weak. But by facing your fears and allowing yourself to share your vulnerability with others, you have become even stronger. This breakdown has catapulted your breakthrough. You are finally free to be your true authentic self and you are inspiring others with your story.

I forgive you for sitting back and waiting for the world to change. In order to see a change, you must take responsibility and be the change. And that is an inside job. By being consciously aware of your thoughts, words, and actions, you have been able to change your perception of the world. Instead of seeing chaos and unrest, you now see clarity and transformation. And by finding the love, light, peace, and joy within, you can now illuminate a path for others.

I forgive you for questioning your self-worth. You and everyone else in this world were born worthy and deserving. Your thoughts are the only thing holding you back from unlimited health, wealth, and abundance. There is no reason to play small. Holding yourself back does not only impact you. It's like throwing a stone into still water; it creates a ripple effect. Whether you know it or not, other people are watching you on your journey through life and it's time to stand proud, own your worth, and be an outstanding role model.

I forgive you for always trying to "fit in" and be "normal." By choosing this path, you denied yourself love and acceptance. And you held your unique gifts captive from the world. You were not born to be ordinary. You were meant to be EXTRAordinary. Being born with vim and vigor is a blessing. Choose to share your effervescence and zeal for life. During these dark times, your light is desperately needed.

I forgive you for not making yourself a priority. By always showing up and pushing through when you had nothing left to offer, you burned yourself out. But this pandemic has allowed you the time and space to realize and embrace that it is OK to be SELFish. You cannot serve or support others until you take care of yourself. Being SELFish means SELF-Love, SELF-Respect, and SELF-Care. And by taking the lead and being SELFish, you have inspired others to do the same.

I forgive you for looking outside yourself and trying to make your dreams come true right away. Just because we live in a world of immediate gratification, does not mean that all your dreams are going to come true in a Bibbidi Bobbidi Boo moment. Your fairy godmother is not going to appear and change your life with a stroke of her wand. If you want magic, you are going to have to go within to find it. To make the magic happen, you need to set an intention, commit to your dreams, take consistent action, and Bibbidi Bobbidi DO YOU!

I forgive you for fixating on what you haven't accomplished yet. It's time to reflect on your past and acknowledge and appreciate everything that you have already achieved and overcome. Your struggles have made you stronger. The challenging situations you have faced have amplified your resilience, courage, and perseverance. Do not criticize your journey. You are exactly where you are supposed to be in this moment.

I forgive you for getting derailed from your spirituality

because of your frustration with religion. God is always present. And whether you call Him God, Universe, Source, Higher Power, or Good Ol' Divine, it's all good. He is just happy to connect with you. It's never too late to reach out. And whether you want to share gratitude or frustration, He appreciates listening and is always ready to help. Just remember that God has big plans for you, and they may not be perfectly aligned with yours. Always keep the lines of communication open so you can receive His messages.

I forgive you for living in a constant state of motion. Going and doing does not mean you are being productive. You need to give yourself a break to just BE in the moment. Step off the hamster wheel and be truly appreciative of the present. It is a magical gift that opens a gateway to unlimited opportunities and possibilities. Give yourself time to rest, relax, and reboot so you can be refreshed and ready to receive. Sometimes the easiest way to lean into your greatness is by slowing down and allowing it time to catch up to you.

I forgive you for being afraid of change and transformation. It can be scary to let go of your limiting beliefs and self-doubts that have guided you through life. But it can be even more frightening and uncomfortable to continue living from your past. Take time to reflect on how far you have already come in life and embrace the fact that you are constantly learning, growing, and evolving. You are a beautiful being and every day you grow more and more becoming.

Unlike a caterpillar, who is unaware of his journey to become a butterfly, it takes a lot of courage for you and other humans to be consciously aware of this dark time in transition from who you once were to who you are becoming. It takes faith, trust and acceptance to allow yourselves to sit in your cocoons and be OK with the unknown. And since transitions are never a one and done, you must learn to see life from a different perspective. From now on, stop fixating on what you are giving up and focus on what you are gaining. God has a BIG plan for you. And your mission is to believe in Him and trust in your unlimited potential.

It's time for you to step confidently out of your cocoon, stretch your magnificent wings, and fly. It's time to look in the mirror and acknowledge and appreciate your greatness and your beauty. Release any fears and worries to your guardian angels and embrace your truth. Your mission is to share your love, light, peace, and joy. Now that you comprehend that life is about the journey and not the destination, share your knowledge with others. Your words of wisdom have healing powers.

Shine bright and illuminate a path for people to follow so they can find the way out of their unconscious conditioning and into conscious awareness. Keep showing up and sharing your authenticity and PositiviDee. People need to know that although they may not be able to choose what happens to them in life, they have absolute control and authority over how they deal with their circumstances and situations. Show others how to live by design and not by default. And be the leader you were born to be.

Create a movement that inspires community and unity. Always seek to understand and be there for others. Everyone is at a different stage in their transformation and you are being called to meet them where they are in this moment. Show others the way to live life by F.A.I.T.H. and not fear because Fundamental Awareness Inspires True Healing.

With Love & Compassion,

Your Higher Self

About Dee

Dee DiFatta is a high-vibe motivational speaker, PostiviDee coach, educator, and author. After 48 years of life, 26 years with multiple sclerosis, and 17 years working in the insurance industry, Dee decided to be true to herself and live her purpose and her passion. Setting herself free with awareness and authenticity, she is no longer allowing her circumstances or outside influences to define her.

Dee is passionate about teaching and inspiring people to find their way out of their own way. She is committed to sharing her love, light, and PositiviDee to illuminate a path for others to find inner confidence and clarity. Dee lives in Ludlow, Massachusetts, with her soulmate, Mike, her talented daughter, Casey, and her German Shepherd, Jackson.

"In order to be truly aligned with the new design you have created for yourself, it's time to start down the freedom trail of forgiveness."

Dee DiFatta

ADoseofPositiviDee.com

Chapter 2

The Journey Back to Me

Melissa Molinero

Today, I woke up knowing that I am blessed! I woke up in paradise, to a beautiful sunset overlooking Miami Beach, as I got ready to return from a 10-day family vacation. I am currently in the middle of buying the home of my dreams and am enjoying realizing another dream of being a published author.

I love what I do as a life and career coach because I get to work with inspiring people every day. My faith in and my relationship with God are nothing short of amazing. I get to share my life with the most wonderful husband and children I could ever have been gifted. Life is good!

Actually, it's way better than good. It's really a dream come true; something I never thought could or would be mine. Even though my dreams continue to unfold before my eyes and I see I have the power to create an out-of-this world reality, things haven't always been this glorious for me. When I think of who I used to be, and who I am today, I see two totally different people. Miracles happen every day, and my life is one of them.

Sometimes, in the quiet, when I think of my past or look in the mirror, I can still see the physical, emotional, and mental scars that shaped my view of the world before I could understand or even verbalize it.

I was 3-years-old when I learned the world wasn't a safe

place and began to believe I had to prove myself worthy of love. I was sitting on the kitchen floor face-to-face with my mom's very old and large mixed-breed dog, Ben. I was talking to him and admiring his cute doggy face when, suddenly, I felt the force of what seemed like a wall knocking me down to the floor. Nearly breathless and unable to move, I realized I was laying in a pool of my own blood, and then the panic set in.

When I mustered the strength to stand, I ran as quickly as I could into the kitchen where my mom was cleaning up after dinner. I couldn't see what she saw and the pain didn't hit me yet. I wasn't crying, but the shock and fear in my mother's eyes said it all. She grabbed me tighter than ever and began to wail from someplace deep inside of her. When I heard her piercing cries I couldn't help but cry, too. Next, I remember my mom grabbing a rag off the counter and trying to stop the blood from gushing while getting ready to take me to the hospital. At that moment I knew this was bad!

I can retell this story as an adult realizing what actually happened. I guess Ben didn't like the high pitched squeaks of my toddler voice as I spoke to him, and he attacked me, leaving three large gashes and two puncture wounds on the right side of my face. The fear that consumed me during the attack was far worse than any pain I felt on my face, and I hadn't even realized the extent of the damage.

The next hard lesson unfolded within seconds when my daddy, the man who I thought would protect me and put me first above all else, refused to take Mom to the hospital while screaming at her about having to work in the morning. My mom didn't have to say a thing. I could see the hopelessness in her face as she tried to hold back the tears and called her cousin who graciously volunteered to help.

I remember asking myself what I had done to make Daddy react the way he did and why he didn't care about what happened to me. I thought it had to be my fault; why else would he turn away from me without a care? That painful rejection felt worse than anything I endured that day. Even worse than that initial breathtaking drop to the floor. In that moment I learned I wasn't important enough to those closest to me, and that I would have to work much harder to make people (especially my people) love me. It wasn't enough just to exist, it wasn't enough just to be, and it sure wasn't enough to be just ME.

When my cousin pulled up to the house, I climbed into the back seat of the car, worried and anxious about what was to come. We got to the hospital, and more anxiety began to flood over me. I had no idea what to expect.

At the time it was 1986, and medical advances weren't like they are today. When we finally got settled into a room, Mom and the doctor said a lot of stuff I didn't understand. Then, everyone started to move really quickly, and voices got louder and more rushed. What happened next was painstaking.

They strapped me to a bed, my hands and feet buckled down. I couldn't move. While I was awake, a team of four surgeons began to poke my face with what seemed like thousands of needles. I thought the pain would never end! I prayed to be back at home in my warm bed.

When it was finally over, I was wrapped with gauze from the top of my head to my shoulders with only my mouth and eyes visible. My face ached, my body shook, and I was sent home looking like a mummy. I said nothing on the way home and remained silent when I got inside the house. My dad was awake by that time and tried consoling me, but I was angry. I stared into space, motionless on the couch feeling a combination of shock, fear, and deep despair that I will never forget.

For years, I endured the constant questioning and bullying of my peers who pointed out my ugly scars and imperfections. I came to accept that I felt ugly and would never look like the other girls. I was also afraid of everything, especially that no one would ever love me. Words of mockery by adults and children made those stories all too real to me. I was the girl nobody wanted to be friends with. I went to great lengths declaring who I really was just so some of my peers would like me. But most of the time I just felt like I was someone everyone only tolerated.

Thoughts of inadequacy and a huge gaping need for self-acceptance and love followed me into my teenage and adult years and manifested in various unfulfilling ways.

When I was 11 my mom moved me and my two sisters out of my dad's house, which was a blessing in a way because I was able to reinvent myself in a new school and town. Unfortunately, I just created another version of me that I thought everyone would like, and further lost myself in the process.

Avoiding, I poured myself into school. I joined several clubs, never got less than an A on assignments, and rose to rank #7 in my senior class. I got accepted to the university of my choice on a full scholarship. I was accomplished, I was smart *and* popular, I was everything I wanted to be for everyone else, and I was completely lost.

In four years of college campus living, I made friends, began to come out of my shell, and started to question what I wanted to do with my life. This was both an exhilarating and frightening time for me because in only a few short years I would actually have to choose what was next for me, and when you really don't know who you are, that is a daunting task. I chose something predictable, something I had been doing for a while in high school. I decided to be a journalist.

Yes, I loved journalism, the writing, the thrill of the story, and the connection I made with people. But, for some reason, I couldn't really see myself in the profession. I pursued it anyway, afraid the bubble I lived in would pop if I actually told people I had no idea what I liked or what I wanted to do with my life. I was so afraid it would reveal how imperfect I was by uncovering the inadequacies I felt my entire life. Talk about a wake-up call!

I had to have it figured out! And, I had to be good at it! Without that, all I could ever be was that ugly little girl that no one loved. The facade kept me relevant and praiseworthy, even if only for a while. I preferred that over facing what was really behind the stories I clung to growing up. I preferred the comfort of remaining in my own predictable bubble of stories and personalities that I could use whenever the perfect situation applied.

Fast forward a few years later. Same story, different year. I never pursued journalism after graduation, and instead worked in a bank for eight years. At 23, I married and became a mom at 24. I loved being a mom! Everything about being important to someone who really needed me was so fulfilling. Finally, I didn't have to try so hard to be special for others because I was special to my baby girl.

I poured my whole self into the mom role, and I lost touch with reality. I stopped relating to myself as a human being with needs, and only saw myself as a mom.

I realize now that the day the dog attacked me, I gave up all the power I had and allowed my fear to run the show for a really long time.

That's the thing about stories. Once you create them in your head, you start developing incidents that build evidence around them, and you get really comfortable living inside of those stories. So comfortable that breaking through them to believe something different seems impossible and even ridiculous.

Five years ago the stories I created as a child suddenly stopped working for me, and I headed down a dark path. I didn't care about anything. I carried on the day-to-day routines, but I was just a body, totally numb, without feeling. I detached myself from my family and befriended people that brought me further away from myself and those I loved. I was so far detached that I couldn't even see a person in myself anymore. All I saw was a shell of the person I used to be; a fragment of the successful woman I was supposed to be.

My life was in shambles. I couldn't put the pieces back together, and no matter how hard I tried to hold on, life escaped me. Days turned into weeks, weeks into months, and I couldn't break the cycle of suffering I felt in my heart and mind. My escape turned into my ruin. My marriage was ending. We fought about everything, anything. There was no connection and I didn't care! I didn't want to fix it.

I sunk so deep into depression that I couldn't see a way out. I sensed a deep mud pit pulling me down with no ladder and no one to bring me up. I was drowning and I didn't want to fight for it anymore. I couldn't deal with the burdens of money issues and our children's needs creating constant guilt and glimpses of failed attempts at doing things better. God seemed a million miles away and totally out of reach.

Then, something changed. Something changed because I

changed. I was riding in the car with my husband one day after work when I asked him to pull over. I dropped to my knees in my grey Honda Odyssey and I cried out to the Lord with the deepest anguish I have ever felt! At first, I didn't even know the sounds were coming out of me, and I prayed aloud for God to save me from myself. That day, my life transformed.

Five years ago I was a totally different person. I hated life and I wanted to give up. My Lord and Savior heard my cries and He saved me. I never looked back. I began regaining parts of myself piece by piece. I started singing again. I joined a church in my community and became a part of the choir. I baptized my children and dedicated them to the church. I fought for my husband, and, little by little, I won his heart back. My kids became my world, and I worked hard to make them see how much I loved them.

Feeling so much love, three years ago I decided to take a chance on myself. I registered for a life coaching course because I wanted better for me and my family. My two goals were to build my own business from the ground up and to finally buy my dream home.

Not only was I able to build my business as a life and career coach, but I am currently buying that dream house I always wanted, my husband and I have a wonderful and loving relationship, my children are thriving in all areas and developing their own talents, I have become a deacon in leadership at my church, I lead worship service on a regular basis, I am a twice-published author, and I help others in their own life journeys.

When I finally surrendered my life to God and took a chance on myself, realizing I was worth much more than I ever believed, my healing began. The breakthroughs leading to my transformation have been endless since.

This is not a one-time fix, though. I continue to work on myself daily because, as a human, I still tend to allow my stories of "not good enough," or "I have to suffer through it," or "I have to do it alone" to run the show. Thankfully, these thoughts are fleeting, and now I am able to see my worth. I love who I am. I accept myself for the good and the bad, and I forgive myself for it all; for everything I was, for everything I wasn't, and for how I treated myself all the years I thought I didn't deserve better.

Despite what happened to me with that dog almost 34 years ago, today I am a proud owner of two huge Rottweilers, and I wouldn't have it any other way!

I know that with the help of God, I was able to pull myself out of that pit and reinvent my life in exactly the way I have always envisioned, not perfect, but completely me.

About Melissa

Melissa Molinero is a strong Christian woman with unwavering faith in God. She is a mom to two beautiful children who mean the world to her, a wife of 13 years to the most supportive and loving husband, and an ordained deacon at Woodcliff Community Reformed Church in North Bergen, New Jersey.

A life and career coach and certified job counselor in the state of New Jersey, Melissa offers individual and group coaching sessions, workshops, and professional résumé writing services. Melissa enjoys singing, reading, writing, community service, nature getaways, and creating events in service of personal growth and leadership development.

"I love who I am. I accept myself for the good and the bad, and I forgive myself for it all; for everything I was, for everything I wasn't, and for how I treated myself all the years I thought I didn't deserve better."

Melissa Molinero

msmcoaching.com

Chapter 3

Putting the Pieces Together

Lynn Gallant

*"Life is a puzzle and once all the pieces
come together it will be and feel complete."*
Breanna Brotherton

How did I get here? How do any of us really?

When most people look at me, I know they would never guess the road I have traveled or the pieces that make me whole. This is the trip I took to arrive here in my power, with the ability to thrive, losing and gaining pieces along the way.

As so many teenage girls growing up in the 70s and 80s, I was extremely insecure. My vision of myself was skewed, thrown off by idyllic visions of movie stars, models in magazines, and pretty petite girls who were constantly reassured and complimented on their appearance. I was *not* one of those girls.

Don't get me wrong. I never struggled with obesity, terrible acne, or horrific disfigurement. But, my body dysmorphia led me to believe I was larger than I was. Could this have been because my taller than average height brought constant remarks and questions like, "Wow, aren't you a Big Girl?" and "Do you play basketball?" "Tall" was always replaced with that horribly awful word "BIG." For a girl led by societal stigma that *small* and *petite* were *good* and *big* was mortifyingly *bad*, these words echoed in my head and messed with my mindset. In addition to always feeling oversized, I never believed myself to be attractive, seeing everything in the mirror as "too." Eyes "too" brown, hair "too" curly, nose "too" big, breasts "too" big, body "too" tall, lips "too" thin. This self-critical vision had a profound impact on my self-esteem, especially living in a household where it was not common to receive compliments on how you looked. I went down a dark road.

Food became the enemy, something to be avoided or kept at a distance like kryptonite. I began to struggle with eating disorders. I would either lose control, binging and purging, or completely deny myself barely more than salad every day. It was a way to punish myself for not being good enough. I was hopeful it could solve one issue, helping me to shrink down to a size of acceptability. Could I attain the cute, small, petite vision that was so seemingly perfect to the world? This vision of "not good enough" became more dangerous when I entered my freshman year in college. I had never had a male admirer much less a boyfriend.

Through my battle with food and eating disorders, I lost weight and became a little more confident, the reverse Freshman Fifteen. My eyes opened to the attentions of the opposite sex, and I liked it. It made me feel special. Wanted. Desired in a way I had never felt. I allowed sexual advances, afraid to say "no" in fear that I would be rejected, not good enough. Promiscuity became a way for me to feel accepted. It was freeing at times, horribly impersonal and invasive at others. I had nothing to compare it to. I had a few casual "relationships" but it took a while to break that cycle of feeling inadequate unless I offered up something others might not. I struggled to understand the difference between intimacy and true love.

After a number of years of playing with fire, and many broken moments, I was able to find what makes me happy and recover from this chapter of my life. Experiencing real life by having a career after college and living on my own helped my growth process. Although I had much help through this stage of my life from many friends and family and some therapists, I give the majority of the credit to meeting my loving husband, my soulmate, who opened my eyes and loved me for the real me. He loved all the pieces of me, regardless of how I felt about each of them, and was so accepting of my negative self-talk and constant need for reassurance. He has kept me on the right path with this unconditional love, and always saw me for who I could truly become. How I was seen in HIS eyes was a reality that began to wake me up and help me to see differently.

I began to head toward a healthier relationship with food, one I had known existed deep down inside of me. I had removed the foods that were triggers for me – fried, unhealthy foods, rich desserts; those I eliminated from ever eating again. It was my safe zone, for now, until I could learn how to live with them harmoniously.

During this time of dysmorphia, I would look at many people in my life, admiring them, wishing I could look like them, envious even, not realizing they were actually 20 pounds heavier and four sizes bigger than I was. When a college friend said to me, "Lynn, try on these pants," to prove to me she was bigger, I tried them on and they fell to the floor. It still didn't register. It must have been the way she carried herself, the confidence she radiated, and how healthy she was that I admired.

My love for knowledge and learning kept me grounded enough to stay in recovery – most of the time. These new

realizations about myself brought about new passions –
explorations into the latest diet or fitness craze. I always learned
the scientific approach behind each of them but never fully
adopted any. It was about learning the pieces of each plan and the
science behind them. Somehow, deep down, I knew it was always
about what was sustainable, long-term. There was a passion
inside me to get to the root of these issues. I wanted to learn, to
help others, and to find sustainable solutions. I stayed strong and
was determined to move forward. Fueling my body with healthier
foods, staying away from triggers, and seeking happiness and
fulfillment in my career put me on a path to build a life of fun,
family, and success. Sounds idyllic, but it's not. It was actually
wrought with resentment at times...mostly people judging me,
feeling that I was extreme or radical in my choices.

Although eating disorders remained in remission through
my child bearing years, my body dysmorphia did not. I was in
full-on "Super Mom" mode, putting everyone else before me. My
health began to suffer with illnesses, exhaustion, and weakness.
After a prolonged illness, I was diagnosed with chronic
Epstein-Bahr. This made me feel inferior, as I was unable to do
my volunteer work at the school, and providing for my family
became a challenge. I had not yet realized that I had the power to
manage this.

It was a wake-up call for me, a time for deep reflection and
emotion. I immediately adjusted my schedule, rested when I was
tired, and altered my eating to include more plant-based
nutrition to heal my body. Yes! Steps in the right direction,
but...not enough of the pieces were put together yet since I was
often sick with minor infections. Questioning and animosity
from those in my family and circle of friends continued as they
wondered if I truly knew what was best for me. They asked,
"What are you eating?" "Are you eating enough?" "Shouldn't you

be eating meat?" The questions were endless.

Years of chronic illness later, I was introduced to Juice Plus+ whole food nutrition. I went from literally falling to pieces almost every month, resorting to medications to recover, missing out on recitals, concerts, meetings, and family outings to being fully functioning, having more energy, actually thriving, becoming strong. I was an example of health rather than the example of illness!

Simple vine-ripened fruits, vegetables, and berries in capsules changed everything. With research to back them up, these capsules reduce oxidative stress, improve immune function, support lung and cardiovascular wellness, and more. If these capsules of 30 vine-ripened fruits, veggies, and berries could make such a difference in my life, I knew they could do so much for others. I began learning about the company's mission of "Inspiring Healthy Living" and knew it was *my* calling, and it would be on *my* time. I devoured all of the education – along with all that I had been collecting throughout my life. I was putting it together and it was making so much sense to me. I was a living example of how one can thrive by making simple, sustainable lifestyle changes.

This road was not a smooth one, but it was mine. I have fallen many times, but continue to get up. I added pieces to my education along the way, including "The Truth About Cancer" series, as I had a non-smoking friend who suffered lung cancer and my sister was going through treatment for metastatic breast cancer. They had each made their choice on how they would fight their fight. In the end, they lost their battles with cancer.

These losses left life-long scars on me but I learned so much from each of them and carry those lessons with me daily. Everyone has a choice in life. Prevention, treatment options, screening choices, lifestyle choices...the list is endless. Sure, I have my opinion, as do most people, on the best path. However, I chose to educate and let the choice be theirs.

Looking back at the transformative stages of my life, I find myself reflecting on how each has been a critical building block, creating what I stand in now – my wholeness. The breakdowns, the recoveries, the celebrations, the stumbles, and the falls are what were absolutely necessary for me to become me, to understand my full purpose in life, and to have the ability to appreciate all I have achieved. Without the journey, there would be no authentic self: the strength that has lived inside of me all along.

Do I still struggle with body dysmorphia now? A bit here and there. I certainly have built quite a toolkit along my journey to wholeness. I have picked up the pieces of me along the way that tell my story and that have made me who I am today. It is those pieces that distinguish me from others. I am originally *me*, and my transformative journey has placed me exactly where I need to be. I am here to help people regain their health, wellness, and wholeness, with the tools I have gained.

The point I would like to make is this: Don't judge what a person can do for you based on their appearance. You do not know of their journey or the tools they have gathered along the way. The key is to listen and to hear the clues in their voice and in their story. Have you been there?

Can you relate? Maybe. Maybe not. But does it inspire you?

The key to my healing was finding my ultimate happiness, the cure for my illnesses, and not settling for failure. This allowed me to open up my mind and my heart to true love and inspiration. The real path to learning, however gradual it may have been, made so much sense when it started to unfold. Did I completely realize it as it was unfolding? Not always. However, I kept the pieces figuring someday I might need them.

Healing is an ongoing process. Wounds can reappear when you least expect them to – drawn out by triggers. As I have grown through the decades, I have collected these broken and some not-so-broken pieces of myself. I have gradually been able to put them together in an order that makes sense and can help others. I have educated myself through programs, organizations, and mentors, and I have aligned myself with amazing communities, friends and family to ensure the healing continues.

Through self-care, good nutrition, a positive mindset, a balanced life, and the sharing of my story I have created wholeness and it's wonderful.

But what was next for *me*? After almost 20 years at this point of stay-at-home-momhood, what would be my purpose? I had an identity struggle. My girls were pretty self-sufficient, yet I wanted to be home if they needed me and my husband's travel schedule was pretty intense. Going back to pharma was out for sure as my belief system in the industry had shifted. And, working outside of the home would take away the time flexibility I so desperately wanted to hang onto.

Since I have a relational quality to me, one of non-judgment, and it is my desire to assist people with what *they* want to work on, I get to the root of what may be their blocks and help people to incorporate real food into their lives without guilt and fear. I also learn what might be standing in the way of their goals. I work with whole food nutrition products that have been proven to improve many systems of the body and I am living proof they work.

But it's not all about products. It's about how you feel, how much energy you have, and how much sleep you are getting. It's about being able to function in ways that you feel are productive and fun...not having reasons to say no that are preventable.

Lifestyle changes are key to putting the pieces together that work, leaving the rest to be recycled or reduced. I liken it to a salad bar – pick and choose what you like and what works, and leave the rest. It's all good but *you* get to choose. It's this type of plan that is sustainable over time. There are so many connections I have made along the way who are there for guidance, support, and assistance. It takes a village, and wholeness is really never about just one thing. It's about the pieces coming together.

About Lynn

Lynn Gallant has been married to John for 24 years and his partner for 30. They have two beautiful, smart daughters together, Jordan and Devin. They are empty nesters kept busy by their two Aussies, Vickie and Tazzy, and Luna the Cat.

Lynn received her degree in hotel hospitality management from Northern Vermont University, and after 10 years working in the hotel industry, has spent her life building on her knowledge in the health, wellness, and fitness fields. She has a strong background in cardiovascular health from her time spent with Novartis Pharmaceuticals and gains much of her current knowledge from the many doctors and wellness professionals at Juice Plus+ and Tower Garden. She recently became certified in health, nutrition, and fitness to solidify her plan to work with clients within these specialties and has added Scout and Cellar Clean-Crafted wine to her portfolio.

"It takes a village, and wholeness is really never about just one thing. It's about the pieces coming together."

Lynn Gallant

lynngallant.com

Chapter 4

A Crack that Let the Light In

Kristina Crooks

Currently, some people are experiencing the hardest times of their lives. If that's you, I'm with you, I see you, I've been there. I promise, with the right support, the right mentors, and the right tribe around you, it can get better. I'm 37-years-old and a California native living in upstate New York with my fiance of five years. Our road together is a whole other story, which I can't wait to share one day. We have four adorable, mischievous kitties, own our home, and love exploring nature. I do my best to not sneak-coach him by remembering one of my favorite acronyms: Let. Others. Voluntarily. Evolve. It's also the way I define Love.

As you journey with me, I hope you take the pieces that feed you, lift you, nourish you, empower you, and, most importantly, resonate with you. Take the pieces that crack you open and lead you to a created, inspired, and powerful life. There may be parts of my story that confront you, upset you, enrage you, or even make you feel sorry for me. Please don't. I urge you to notice how you feel and embrace any edges that come up. Navigating the shards of my own pain has developed me into someone who generates a deep, divine LOVE, wherever I am, because the other side of deep pain and trauma is deep love and grace. I hope you witness my story with compassion for all the people involved, because they have their own story, their own traumas, and their own epigenetic markers, just like I have mine. We are all human, doing the best we can with the tools we have.

I trained as an ontological coach under a true master and couldn't wait to be the same invitation to others as he was for me. A little over a year ago I created Empowered Human LLC, a coaching and consulting company. Every week I get to co-create new realities with clients and potential clients, I get to work with people who inspire me, and I get to interview people who move me to be my best. I wake up every morning and enjoy a cup of coffee while I take a mental note of what I'm grateful for, and breathe in all the love that that generates. But it wasn't always this way.

My childhood was traumatic and surrounded by addiction and mental illness, not my own. There was generational and first-hand trauma. There were epigenetic markers that predetermined how I would likely respond to certain events and my A.C.E.s (Adverse Childhood Experiences) score was 6 out of 10, with an additional 2 on the fence. Before 16, I was a high school dropout that regularly smoked marijuana, drank alcohol, lost my virginity, was raped, and tried meth. I wasn't a winning racehorse going places.

In some kind of paradoxical world, by 19, I had restarted high school, graduated with honors, taught Choice Theory to teachers and administrators, wrote for the school newspaper, ran a culture club, and was recognized for leadership in my school district. When I headed to college and shared my story with a few professors, they were astonished that I could do so well when I had experienced so much trauma and tragedy. It was my version of getting high: excellence, awards, being noticed. I built a facade that made it seem like everything was working out, when really, all I had done was learn to work my ass off, please authority, and be whatever people wanted me to be. I couldn't handle criticism, exclusion, or dislike. So, rather than creating my life I was being created BY life and defined only by the opinions of others. I was building beliefs and behaviors on a rocky foundation that looked like depth and self-reflection but it wasn't; and I wouldn't realize that until I faced divorce at 30. My house of cards would fold in on itself when the person I devoted my life to and drew all of my self-esteem from told me I was worthless. My former husband traveled extensively as a videographer for large music tours and this was his second big world tour. He had been my best friend for 10 years, always had my back, and could make anything hilarious. We could easily keep each other entertained without needing anyone else. We were planning a family while he was settling in to a new well-paying job. I was gearing up to finish my bachelor's degree, and we had just found out I was pregnant after trying for a year and going through a miscarriage. By July 6, 2013, my life was the best I had ever known it to be. I thought I got lucky at my hand in life and I deserved it. I went to bed feeling blessed and a little nervous about becoming a parent myself.

The next day, July 7, I discovered three months' worth of emailed love letters between my husband and his co-worker. Some were even right after he had emailed me. She weighed in on baby names and couldn't wait to be the "auntie" to our child. They had no intention of ever ending their clandestine affair and were planning to align their tours as much as possible. According to him, she was the love of his life.

I was shocked, devastated, and quickly unraveling. I started to put the pieces together...the odd behavior when he was home, the constant texting between them that felt awkward; the signs were there, and I missed them. I called him incessantly to explain himself. I made damaging Facebook comments. I was unhinged. When he finally answered my calls he told me he never loved me, he thought I was fat and gross, and that he didn't want the baby. I couldn't breathe. I felt like I was suffocating and my world was closing in on me. This couldn't be happening! How could this be true? Was I truly unlovable? How could 10 years be a lie? Did he marry me out of pity? Am I that pathetic? I was spiraling in an undertow of dense emotion. He refused to come home and the tour didn't end for another two weeks.

The next two weeks were the longest of my life. I oscillated between panic, rage, debilitating grief, physical pain, and nausea. I felt like my body was being ripped to shreds, and now I had to make life-altering choices that I didn't ever think I would face. My eyes were so puffy I looked like I had been stung by a hundred bees. I would stand in front of the mirror and try to drag my self-esteem out of the gutter, but all I could hear were his stinging words over and over and over. I wanted my life back, I wanted my husband to love me, I wanted to have our baby in the idyllic way I had imagined. But none of that was true anymore, and, it turns out, none of that was my path. Sometimes everything needs to be destroyed for something new to grow.

I began packing his things and stuffing them into his car. I was running on inner rage and adrenaline which, unbeknownst to me, was also my drug then. I filed for divorce at the end of the month. I booked a flight to upstate New York to see my family and volunteer at a personal growth institute for a month. I sublet my place in beautiful Santa Cruz, California. I made peace with the gentle soul growing inside of me, and at eight weeks I said goodbye. Terminating a pregnancy was never an option I thought I would need to face, but I didn't want her to be born into this mess. I could barely take care of myself, let alone provide a healthy environment as a single mother with no job or income.

Within a month, I was flying to the Option Institute to make something better out of my living hell. There were days I just knelt in my room and sobbed; for the life I wouldn't have, for the child I wouldn't raise, for the loss of everything I knew only a month before. But it was also the beginning of learning a different way of being. It was the beginning of learning that the intersection between philosophy, science, and psychology could begin to explain why I had built a foundation in a glass house. I didn't know the term ontology then, but I was planting the seeds to become an ontological coach. My ex-husband and I were mirror images of one another that kept trying to fix and coddle each others' pains. We called that love. This was the beginning of building a life on the sacred ground of truth, authenticity, and integrity. There was no going back.

For the next seven years I hunted for answers. I was clear how quickly life could take a sharp left, which also inspired the thought that if it could get exponentially worse, it could get exponentially better. It reminded me to appreciate where you are and to never put your self-esteem in the hands of another, good or bad, because it's a dangerous game of Russian Roulette. I had created a mask of how I wanted the world to see me so I could get my needs met. That very way of being was my Achilles heel. I never wanted to be that compartmentalized again.

I went to conferences like Wisdom 2.0 and Emerging Women. I volunteered at retreat centers like 1440 Multiversity. I went on retreats with speakers and authors I admired. I took courses in organizational leadership and the brain and human behavior. I built a tribe that was willing to call me out and I sought out mentors that were skilled in reparenting. I began running business development operations for a special needs school, which was all about studying behavior. I even walked on fire in the middle of downtown Denver, Colorado, while surrounded by drums and 250 other women. I had a voracious appetite to learn and learn and learn. A thirst that was never quite quenched, much like an athlete that is never satiated with their performance. I was mastering doing, but not being.

By 35, I finally went inward for answers. I hired an executive coach to train me in ontology and invested in transformational programs like Landmark; I joined a mastermind group and a spiritual center; I sought out leaders whose basement was my ceiling. I joined 12-step groups that allowed me to process my childhood traumas. I co-created a new relationship with an incredible man, I moved across the country, I purchased my grandfather's home, and I went full-time in my business. Things began to shift in ways I had never experienced before, and I finally let myself really be seen.

I no longer draw my self-esteem from others, but it doesn't mean I'm a fan of upsetting others. Sometimes I say things I need to clean up, but it's far less frequent. I'm no longer trapped in the lie of unworthiness or shame or hustling to be noticed. I'm no longer fueled by rage, pain, or grief, but I still experience them and allow them to flow through me. Sometimes I need to be sad, pissed, or upset but I no longer abuse myself for it. I get to live in what's possible rather than what has happened. Most of all, it means an unshakable amount of self-love and compassion.

This is just a glimpse of my story, a piece that created incredible transformation in my life. I invite you to find ways to consciously fall in love with your life. To be willing to go within, and face yourself. There is so much waiting for you here.

About Kristina

Kristina Crooks is professionally trained as an ontological coach and the founder of Empowered Human, a coaching and consulting firm.

Before building her own company, she worked for a variety of small businesses to build their revenues and client base. As a result, she is able to identify what's missing, what's next, and what's possible.

She lives in upstate New York with her fiancé and is a virtual member of Toastmasters, Center for Spiritual Living, and a mastermind based in Switzerland.

"Navigating the shards of my own pain has developed me into someone who generates a deep, divine LOVE, wherever I am, because the other side of deep pain and trauma is deep love and grace."

Kristina Crooks

kristinacrooks.com

Chapter 5

Take the Shot

Noelymari Sanchez Velez

Everything you have gone through has been preparing you for this very moment. A moment of transformation, a moment that made possible all the connections you have made to make you who you are today.

Transformation is defined as a metamorphosis, a change during a life cycle, an action that is to be taken. During our life we go through many transformations without realizing it and they all prepare us for that pinnacle moment that you have been praying for.

There was a time in my life when I felt that I needed to make a change, a transformation like no other. For many years my internal voice was quiet. At times I did not know if this was the way life was meant for me, if I was settling. We sometimes do not understand that we are in a situation of struggle and unhappiness. We simply accept it and feel this is the way life is supposed to be.

I have always been a planner, a To Do lister, and when you have no control of where your life is heading, you feel completely lost. It was an emotional torture not knowing where I stand, and this took its toll on me. I started gaining weight and, although I was confident with myself, I was just not happy. I was at a crossroads and did not know what direction to take. My breaking point was having the courage to see beyond all of this and wanting to have a life where I could be happy and allow myself to flourish.

In search of my purpose and what I would do next, I started submerging myself in learning new things, getting out of my comfort zone, reading more diverse topics, and looking for guidance on how to move forward in life. One of the many books I was reading that made a huge impact on me was "The Voice of Knowledge" by Don Miguel Ruiz. The writer makes it a point for the reader to feel worthy and that no matter what they have been conditioned to feel, they are perfect beings. We are perfectly and wonderfully created, and we deserve to feel valued, respected, and supported.

I made it my mission to better myself externally to understand what my body really needed. Losing weight has not always been easy for me. On top of having issues with my hormones, I needed the appropriate guidance and discipline to embark on this phase of my transformation. I sought the help of a naturopath and also became part of an amazing fitness tribe that helped me achieve my goals. It was then that I learned how to make the spirit, mind, and body connection. This connection provides the clarity and spiritual guidance to focus your mind and allow your body to ignite the process.

Wanting to lose that extra weight was part of my story, but the liberation of what was holding me back, to find my voice, to take action, to understand myself, and to be able to inspire others along the way are what my transformation was about. Connecting your spirit and mind to make any decision is a way to allow yourself to LET IT ALL GO; the process to lose that emotional weight that is holding you back.

Growing up in a Christian home and family, I have

experienced how powerful it is to have God in my life. As I got older, being able to understand what was meant for me has truly made my relationship with Him stronger. I truly understand and have personally experienced that no matter what you go through in life, we are protected and what is meant for you will be manifested. According to the scriptures in Ecclesiastes 3:1-8 we have been "appointed time for everything, a time for every activity under the heavens." May we use this time we have been appointed under the heavens to live purposefully with our gifts and talents to feel divinely fulfilled. Are you allowing for this to be fulfilled in your life?

I remember my trainer's words that I carry with me, "Don't think about it, just do." For two years after that, that is what I did and continue to do, the work, to workout and achieve my goal weight. I felt empowered and confident. I won transformation of the year, continued to maintain my goal weight, and was an inspiration to other women who were searching to do the same, speaking to them about what to do, how to do it and working out alongside them. My work of service to others was really a delight to experience. I was being prepared to face doors that would open for opportunities I would have never imagined.

When were this plan and these opportunities to be presented? I did not know. I did not want to question it or to feel impatient; that is not what this process is about. I challenge and encourage you to take the chance to put into action what you have been putting off doing, to "Just Do."

What was key to my healing was the understanding of what I wanted to do with my life, continuing to understand the spirit, mind, body connection, gaining additional confidence to experience this journey, and to be able to help others along the way. The process of a transformation teaches you to be gentle with yourself, to trust, and to love yourself again - or to love yourself for the first time.

I often listen to women tell me, "I can't do that. I'm not worthy of that. I don't think I'm beautiful enough." STOP IT!!! We are all capable; we are beautiful in our own way. Having confidence in what you do breeds beauty that we all possess. If you really want something, if you have dreamed of wanting to do something with your life, do it. Take the shot. Trust me when I tell you, you will have the right people in your corner, the right connections who will cheer you on, who will believe in you and support you. But it starts with you breaking from what you are used to, understanding what no longer serves you, and growing from it.

I always listen to the signs, paying close attention to how and why others were reaching out wanting to know how I was doing. This allowed me to connect with them, to trust, to open up, and to talk about what I was experiencing. Sometimes we are afraid to tell others our story and our truth for fear of judgment and not being understood. When you are true to yourself and authentic in your journey, your energy will dictate who it will bring closer to you and who will also walk away from you. And that is OK, too.

I learned to take chances, to set goals, and to accomplish them. Many of us are afraid to take the next steps in what we want to accomplish. Take the shot!

Spending more than 20 years in the nonprofit world, I have worked hard in achieving many personal and professional development opportunities, allowing me to grow as a professional by setting different goals and accomplishing them. I have been able to connect with my team by being dependable and leading with passion. This has taught me to take risks, to feel empowered when making decisions. How very grateful I am for these opportunities that have opened doors for me.

Your journey and my journey are different, but yet the same. It doesn't matter how long it takes you and how many are by your side. The point is to believe in yourself, to trust the process and the plan. The journey I took trained me physically and mentally and, even today, transformations continue to happen organically.

The lyrics of the song *Haven't Seen It Yet* by Danny Gokey have stayed with me:

"Have you been praying and you still have no answers? Have you been pouring out your heart for so many years? Have you been hoping that things would have changed by now? Have you cried all the faith you have through so many tears? Don't forget the things that He has done before and remember He can do it all once more..."

You will be given the strength to accomplish anything. Imagine it, walk with action and purpose, and you will experience what you have asked for.

If I had to relive this life again I would, most definitely, but what I wish I knew at certain times in my life is to not procrastinate, to know my worth, and the rest will follow. Go and be where you are wanted, where you are celebrated, and supported.

When you have trusted the journey you have taken and are prepared to continue to DO the work, you will find opportunities to help others along the way. My work in the photography world has allowed me to do just that.

Stand in front of the camera of life, smile, and prepare for a glorious future. Like photography, your life is an art.

This was my experience when I was being photographed for

the first time by my now husband. I felt happy, I felt free, I felt beautiful. I had accomplished my weight loss and I had always wanted to be professionally photographed. This is the beauty of the work we do in our business; we have personally experienced many aspects of our photography. We offer a unique perspective to our clients. We are able to provide them with the tools to look their best and to celebrate who they are.

Through our wedding photography we are building relationships with the families we work with, understanding their needs, and allowing them to enjoy their beautiful celebration. Weddings have always held a special spot in my heart. They evoke happiness, joy, promise, and commitment. As a wedding officiant, I am able to witness the joys of marriage with our clients. Being able to talk about the beautiful union of two individuals and share this with their loved ones allows for more love to fill our world.

Working with the community and capturing their essence, we feel another level of how transformative our photography work is. We have met and worked with individuals who have been affected by tragic loss, trauma, who have promoted peace in their community, who have wanted to find a forever home or celebrated their business. To be trusted to tell their stories is truly an honor and privilege. These are the beautiful connections we make that we will carry with us forever.

When my husband and I first started working together, we did not know how important our connection was going to be in aiding what is now our photography business and what would become our lives together. Working alongside my husband is one of my greatest joys. We get to share our creativity, allowing space for our clients to feel confident and beautiful.

Allow yourself to feel, to be blessed with the bonds you form along your journey, to have people by your side you can trust and who will give you the confidence to bring out the beauty you already possess.

"Never take anything for granted. Never take unconditional love for granted. Never take your health for granted. Never take time for granted. It's all a privilege."
Oglala Lakota

It is my hope that you have felt inspired and moved to take the next step to transform your life, to live your best life, and to make new connections to help you grow.

Namaste mi gente!

About Noely

For the last three years, Noelymari Sanchez Velez has worked with her husband, Julio, as owners of JCV Freelance Photography, LLC, based out of East Hartford, CT. She is the public relations director and wedding officiant and is in charge of customer service and contracts, and "day of" coordination. She and her husband engage in a healthy lifestyle by staying active along with sharing a mutual love for photography and chasing sunsets.

She has more than 20 years of experience at a 145-year nonprofit criminal justice agency based out of Hartford, CT. For the last 18 years, she worked as the executive assistant and project manager, and currently serves as the business operations administrator.

"I learned to take chances,
to be able to set goals and accomplish them.
Many of us are afraid to take the next step
in what we want to accomplish.
Take the shot!"

Noelymari Sanchez Velez

jcv-pics.com

Emerge

out
essence
adventure

Chapter 6

1984

Angel Johnstone

It was the 80s, a time of big hair and bigger lust with rock and roll sexy opulence in all directions. It was when boys looked like girls and the girls LOVED it. It was plastic Madonna bracelets and lace gloves. It was bedroom walls covered completely with pictures of Duran Duran. It was Twisted Sister telling us to ROCK and Motley Crew singing about strip clubs. It was General Hospital every afternoon and a feeling that if Luke and Laura could fall in love then ANYTHING was truly possible. It was HammerTime in Hammer Pants with The Bangles singing "Walk like an Egyptian" and a chorus of kids singing "I Want My MTV."

Music had taken over our world, our culture, our language, and cable TV piped ALL of it in. The sex, the scandal, the sounds and extravagance of the rock and roll stage, and ... the videos. Oh God, the videos! Dancers heaving and heavy breathing. New moves we could use in our neon leg warmers. Hair spray by the case and a free-for-all of Sex, Drugs, and Rock and Roll before Tipper Gore got her parental advisory warning on everything.

I was 12 at this time and pleasantly adrift in a sea of sex and androgyny. My hair and my hope witnessing a high time in the world of fashion, money, and boldness. I survived junior high with best friends, A and J. I survived the unrequited love affair I had with Andrew and the crush I had on the charismatic music teacher. I survived gym class and my first period. And I think, like many of you, I learned about sex from the soap operas and from the neighborhood kids telling me what they knew. (How much did they know? NOTHING). Then I found my dad's *Playboy* and *Penthouse* collections stored in the bottom of his Craftsman roll cart out in the garage, and nothing was ever the same!

So in the summer between 7th and 8th grade, when I was all braces and awkward and full of crazy ideas and crazier hormones, I met new friends from the next neighborhood over. I had the freedom of my bicycle and being a latchkey kid while my mom worked. I rode to their houses and we ate mayonnaise sandwiches on Wonder white bread and dreamt about high school. We swam in the pool and lay in the sun and peddled to the store to buy snacks and watched the soaps and had sleepovers and made big plans for our lives. N, K, L, and I made a summer camp for ourselves out of backyards and living rooms. I felt sisterhood for the first time and it was warmer and richer than ANYTHING I had ever known.

In July, *Purple Rain* hit the theaters and it was the beginning of my love affair with a small light brown man I never met that persists to this day. He told me gender and color and money didn't matter and sex was a religious experience. His music pulsed through my veins forevermore. My friends and I convinced our parents to take us to see that movie over and over and over again. The whole rest of that summer was a haze of purple awesomeness that blended into the start of high school. I worried if my lace gloves, felt hats with veils, and corset tops were cool enough or if my hair was worthy because it wasn't properly full of Aqua Net. Mean Girls were everywhere and the boys were emboldened to leer at my new cleavage. I joined choir and color guard and hung out with the band geeks and drummers (the epitome of musical coolness) and doodled the song lyrics of *Darling Nikki* on book covers and notebooks while trying to navigate the social cues of high school.

That fall I fell HARD into the rabbit hole of young love. We were 13 and I was horny as hell and it was all hot breath and fervent hands, stolen moments, and longing looks. Do you remember how it was? Ahhh... It was as innocent in its unfolding as it was melodramatic. It was fraught with disaster as we were sure to get caught. But it was undeniably exciting, and I wanted MORE. But I was so confused about what to do, or not do, and I went to the guidance counselor for some advice... that's what they do, right? Listen and advise and keep it all safe from the mean girls and the leering eyes. They reserve judgment of my teenage angst. They defend against the threat of constant comparison.

Only this is 1984, and what I am about to say to my guidance counselor, who is 50-something years old, she is not ready to hear.

I say, "I'm in love, but I'm scared because it feels crazy and I don't know what to do with myself. I think about her all the time."

I am so busy talking in a torrent of words that I have finally said out loud, that I don't notice her face change. I don't see the social cue that tells me I misspoke and when she asks me who HE is, I explain that she is my best friend and she is scared, too, and can you please help us figure out what to do next because we love each other so much and don't want to mess it up.

She asks if I could go and get her, my best friend, and maybe we can talk it out together. So I do and we do and we are all impish grins and vibrating nervousness and jittery excitement at our story of touching hands in the movie theater while watching *Purple Rain* for the millionth time and realizing that our friendship was something else. She stays calm and professional and asks a few questions and gives us some parting words that all will be fine and sends us back to class. In the excitement of telling SOMEONE, we float back to class after a stolen kiss in the hall.

What happens next has all the nightmarish betrayal of the soap operas we loved so much. Our parents are called. There is a meeting by day's end. We are screamed at and told this is wrong. We were wrong. There are follow-up meetings planned. There are anger and tears and threats of "don't come near her" and a harrowing car ride home that no matter how hard I try, I do not remember as it is locked deep in my psyche.

What I do remember that afternoon is the yelling and the sobbing and the door slamming and the little ceramic knick knacks that fell off the wall being hurled into my room, into me. Clearly I was too much.

I remember the sleepless night. I remember clutching my teddy bear. I remember feeling completely alone.

And then I remember knowing that my love was feeling the same way. And that knowing made me less alone.

I was in love at 13. Definitely.

I know that as surely as I know that a large part of me, my childhood, died that day. And I know it as surely as I know that another part of me was born.

I spent the next four years in hiding. I was pretending that I was not in a romantic relationship with my best friend. We had boyfriends because it was expected. We were able to spend time together because we became masterful at the art of deception. Our friends aided and abetted this charade with elaborate plans that allowed us to gather at their houses instead of ours. Eventually, our parents bought the story. With one notable exception from our bowling league, we lied to every adult we encountered until we got to college. Stepping "into the closet" was a transformation of a good-hearted, fun-loving, gregarious kid into a teen grappling with a loss of safety and security and a requirement to be other than who she was.

To be clear, this is not the way I recommend anyone advise a teen to travel those formative years! I wish I had known how things would work out back then. I was so fearful that my whole life would be like those years in hiding. It felt so heavy to have to think and rethink every sentence before I said it. Change every pronoun in my head. Worry about if my cover story was elaborate enough. Think about what bits of information my friends need to know to help me avoid enemy detection. I probably would have made an excellent spy! I often wonder how different my life would have been had I not been forced into a cocoon to survive.

But just like a butterfly, I waited and grew in my hiding place until the conditions were right to break free. In college, I joined the LGBTQ+ organization on campus and made friends that I still have today. I became the president of that organization and spoke against discrimination at campus functions and even on cable TV. I found my voice and used it to help others feel safe. I taught the incoming freshman classes that it was now safe for them to "find their tribe." I transformed again – this time into an out and proud lesbian and civic advocate. And when my seven-year relationship ended, it was largely because I had emerged and she needed to remain in her cocoon much longer.

I had enjoyed several relationships with women and worked for the LGBTQ+ community after college when I realized there was a part of me unexplored. A curiosity that was yet to be investigated. So, I transformed again. I granted myself permission to date men. This rocked my gay community friends to the core. They were not ready to accept me as bisexual. My high school sweetheart, upon finding out, even suggested that I had lied to her about who I was during all our years together! I'll be honest - that one stung the most.

To lose my community over my love or desire for "something different" has been a repeating pattern. And, in retrospect, a huge gift. I learned early that growing up and growing emotionally sometimes requires an overhaul of your circle of influence. The people you start with may not be the support system you need in the next phase of your journey. Loving them where they are but continuing your path might be the hardest part of any personal transformation. We want our friends along for the ride but some of them simply aren't ready to embark on that trip with us.

I have found this pattern repeated in careers both corporate and entrepreneurial. I have seen it happen in friendships and intimate relationships. I have witnessed it in the lives of those around me as they grow and change over time. In my experience, I have tried to leave most bridges unburned. Sometimes those old friends come around. They are the ones happy to see you happier.

Ultimately, I have come to believe that growth – whether financial, spiritual, sexual, intellectual, or any other way – is a journey that we take for ourselves. It cannot be done in a vacuum as the relationships in each phase of our learning are required for the growth to happen. However, the societal expectation that every person we meet on that journey is here for the rest of the ride may be unrealistic at best.

So often when we come to the end of a career, business, friendship, or relationship, it is sad, even heartbreaking at times. We often cannot see that a transformation has taken place. Either we have grown, or they have.

As I think about what it means to me to be a coach or a mentor, the fundamental premise is that I am there to help someone transition from where they are today to where they want to be. I get the privilege of believing in their future self when they are still unsure of who that person is. This role is one that can be intimate and personal, but it is also temporary. As each person reaches a new level, they may need a new coach to get them there. My job is to help them get to a place where "letting go" means it is simply time to level up to a new circle of influence and prepare for the next transformation. It is time to come out of the cocoon.

About Angel

Angel Johnstone is an erotica author and writer of short stories for women. She creates confidence-building programs and events by molding together her diverse work background with her love of personal development strategies. Angel started ConfidenceIsCatchy.com and her Facebook page of the same name to bring inspiring ideas and confidence-building resources together. Angel uses her love of public speaking and performance to inspire women to come out of their comfort zone. She recently moved her efforts online to help women find community and sisterhood while exploring pleasure and purpose during COVID-19.

Direct, down-to-earth, and practical, Angel helps women who are searching for no nonsense solutions find fun ways to grow into their future. Her mission is to help women feel more confident so that they can change the world together!

"I learned early that growing up and growing emotionally sometimes requires an overhaul of your circle of influence."

Angel Johnstone

ConfidenceIsCatchy.com

Chapter 7

The Unknown is Not the Enemy

Lori Raggio

Picture a curious 4-year-old child, full of energy, dressed in a cheerleading outfit, saddle shoes and pigtails, with no faculties to understand or make meaning of when bad things happen to good people. Plagued by asthma and kidney infections, she endured frequent hospitalizations before she turned 6.

Her body was maturing rapidly, and she was given experimental shots to stunt her growth to prevent her from having her menstrual period at age 7. Now 10, she weighed 133 pounds, stood 5'3" and felt extremely uncomfortable in her own skin. Boys were interested in her sexually and she lost her virginity at an early age. She attempted to gain control of her body by controlling her intake and quickly she fell to 85 pounds. She would sit at the kitchen table arguing vehemently with her parents over drinking a glass of milk. Constant movement and exercising were her daily focus.

One day her exasperated parents, not knowing what else to do, took her to a psychiatrist who asked her if she wanted to die and that day at that moment MY answer was no. This is my story.

I continued in outpatient therapy to treat my anorexia and to work with a nutritionist to drink Ensure shakes with lots of ice.

Slowly I began to add food, and gained energy and self-confidence as my anorexia continued through college.

From grade school to college, I was a straight-A student, involved in numerous activities searching for where I belonged like marching band, jazz band, student government, color guard, track, student newspaper, residence life, and I graduated from college in five years with two majors and a minor. I learned that this ability to control my body worked in other areas of my life, and I started controlling my time, my relationships, my schedule, my feelings, etc. I learned that attempting to be perfect and looking "put together" on the outside with an energy level of the "Energizer bunny" helped me to avoid someone asking how I was doing or expecting me to be vulnerable.

My commitment to control led to my fierce independence and mistrust in letting others support me, even God. Fear, not abundance, ruled my decisions. To me, success meant working hard, long hours, and prioritizing work first. I was a workaholic. This pattern of behavior resulted in acknowledgment, praise, awards, promotions, etc.

Yet, something was missing inside. I was emotionally exhausted, unfulfilled, and unhappy. I had been living within my comfort zone which prevented me from accessing the endless opportunities that existed in the unknown. My identity was equivalent to my job, title, accomplishments, not the core of who I was or my authentic self, my essence.

For more than two decades this resulted in a highly-respected successful career and yet inside I was lonely. I was living on a hamster wheel looking for the Next Big Thing, chasing shiny objects and wondering why I was not satisfied. I continued this path of overdoing which, in turn, led to others underdoing, a pattern that overshadowed my career and my marriage for 31 years.

Five years ago, I got a glimpse of what it meant to not be able to control life when my mom, my best friend, died at a young 76, only four months after she was diagnosed with two forms of leukemia. I will always remember her last words which she said to me in private, "Lori Annie, you are so beautiful. Am I in heaven?" I stood by her side as her soul left her body when she looked up at the ceiling in her hospice room, reached out her arms, and called to her mom. About six hours later her body left this earth and joined her soul.

The loss of my mom left a deep hole in my life and was a major impetus for my transformation. I felt she was taken from us way too soon and certainly at a time in her life when she was taking care of herself rather than others and adventuring out into the world and reclaiming her life. Her death led me to question God, and my level of spirituality at the time was not strong.

Today, I consider my mom to be, in essence, a midwife in my life. She helps me daily to birth my new creations, and I believe that there is reciprocal healing occurring between us. I have upleveled my spirituality to continue interacting with her at her same spiritual level.

Three years ago, I was downsized from my comfortable HR executive position about one month shy of 16 years of service. Stripped of a title or daily routine, I was forced to slow down, to evaluate who I was, what options I had, what was important to me, and how I wanted to spend my time and energy and utilize my talents. I went from being the breadwinner in my family to taking early deferrals from my 401k to supplement my income while starting a business. This crisis led to a transformation that quietly lurked in the background for many years and for which I am forever grateful.

During my transformation, I went from being a guarded woman with armor to protect me from myself and others to a guardian of sacred space and energy shifts for me and my clients. As the guarded woman, I could be described as: controlling, fearful, protective, driven, ego-knowing, an expert, a doer, a problem solver, and someone possessing a scarcity mindset.

Now these skills, talents, and experiences that helped me in the past but no longer serve me are kept in a royal blue and gold velvet trimmed ornate box that sits on a shelf in my office where they are honored and preserved. As the guardian, I now describe myself as a woman who is open, abundant, flowing, interdependent, vibrant, purposeful, powerful, intentional, dynamic, aligned, spiritual, observant, trusting, being and becoming, an experimenter, reunited with my body and soul, and possessing soul and heart-based knowing.

As I was experiencing my own thresholds of change, I wanted to be fully expressed and alive. I wanted to move from the lone wolf in control who is unable to be truly vulnerable and be able to release commitment to control so that I could access my magic and freedom. I learned this was not possible in full integrity because I was not aligned with my purpose and passions.

During the past two years I intentionally chose to focus on what my soul was being called to do. I was an expert on doing so I searched for a coaching program that focused on "being and becoming." I became an ontological leadership coach via Accomplishment Coaching where I learned to facilitate the immensely powerful Essence Conversation that I now use to help women move from their comfort zone which includes fears, feelings, self-defense mechanisms, and chasing "perfect moments" to a space safe for fulfilling their aspirations. Without practices and rituals in place, our fears suck us back into our comfort zone, robbing us of what our soul desires.

The Essence Conversation is so powerful and is an essential part of any awakening and personal growth journey. It is a tool for inner and outer transformation. The process results in an uncovering of blind spots, enhanced clarity, courage to step into who you must become, and a description of your authentic self which is used to design and develop an aligned personal and professional brand and a prescription for showing up successfully in life. Some client examples include: shaman, sunshine, soul, spark, strength, sanctuary, grace, heart, spirit, energy, beauty, adventure, magnetism, intuition, authenticity, play, flow, sensuality, intrigue, and vibration.

Shortly after becoming a solopreneur, I engaged in a nine-month Ignatian spiritual program to find my core purpose and learn to trust Source. Moving from my comfort zone which involved my fears of "not enough" and imposter syndrome, I learned to despise frenetic pace, to enjoy watching the cactus bloom, to thank Source for the unworldly sunrises and sunsets, to get to know me and to appreciate my body, to put rituals and practices into place to support the guardian instead of the guarded woman. This would not have been possible without the assistance and guidance from coaches and my spiritual advisor who held space for me and supported me as I paused and learned to create appropriate boundaries, reflect, redefine and renew; only then could I take fierce action.

Participating in a year-long transformational retreat leader program culminated in me realizing that to truly help my clients transform I desired to be in stronger alignment with my purpose and guided by Source. I was tired of feeling frustrated and stuck.

I was ready to surrender and release the illusion that control was benefiting me.

On December 26, 2019, I told my husband of 31 years that I wanted a divorce. I sold my home of 21 years in seven days during COVID-19 and moved from Maryland to Arizona, which my soul had been calling me to do for the past 15 years. These changes took strength, vulnerability, trust, and a true belief that my life was capable of expansion.

I learned I have a continuous stream of life force energy and I am a powerhouse. I now use this energy more intentionally and with discernment in order to wait and act at the right time, trusting my own pace. I have incorporated daily rituals of self-care that include meditation, exercise, healthy eating, coaching, spiritual guidance, retreats, energy clearing, and circles of powerful women friends and colleagues.

The impact I am having on my clients includes: new insights whether they are new to the personal growth field or seasoned lifelong learners; courage to embrace oneself and to take initial steps to defining a future self; a deeper level of calm, confidence, and self-acceptance; detachment from outcomes and expectations; and strengthened spirituality. My clients have emerged, grown, and expanded during COVID and are looking forward to opportunities as they create their futures one conversation and one step at a time.

Are you ready to design the life you desire and deserve vs. living by default? Do you feel your Soul calling you, or a deep knowing that there is more to life than what you are experiencing? Are you ready to expand and emerge into something extraordinary? Are you ready to remove your armor?

If you want to uplevel your life and move outside of your

comfort zone, now is the time! During this global pandemic and collective pause the unknown is not the enemy. The unknown is where endless possibilities live. Now is the time for internal evaluation, for renewal and rejuvenation, for taking a stand on what you believe and about what you feel most passionately.

You do not need to know all the answers; you simply need to take the first step and trust that you will be guided to take additional steps that will lead to expansion and abundance.

Using personal connection and deep listening, I partner with women to create new ways of thinking and new ways of seeing the world based on expansion, opportunity, and endless possibilities. My use of powerful provocative questions, silence, radical presence without judgment, intuition, and serious experimentation (play!) in coaching sessions results in breakthroughs, transformation, healing, and committed actions. Together in partnership, I help women focus on what the world of tomorrow needs that they uniquely can provide, and we explore this through engaging in the Essence Conversation, Core purpose work, Alignment of intellect, heart and spirit, and physical movement.

I hope you feel inspired to embark on your own transformational journey. The 4-year-old girl in pigtails who lost herself for many decades found in herself the fierce independence to understand her worth and stop using perfectionism and overdoing to mask her loneliness and low self-esteem. Today she is free, Source is her business partner, and she is the guardian of greatness and opportunities. Her personal transformation is ongoing, and the impact she is having on her clients is incredible. She encourages you to trust in Source, take incremental steps toward your dreams, and listen to your heart and soul.

About Lori

Lori Raggio, MBA, founder and CEO of Inspire Greatness Coaching and Consulting, LLC, serves as the creation catalyst, soul activist and idea generator helping women leaders remove their armor, find their authentic self, and live aligned with their passion and purpose.

She is a compassionate, innovative, strategic, and results-oriented leadership coach, organizational consultant, and transformational retreat leader. She is powered by purpose, driven by insatiable curiosity, and guided by Source to partner with women leaders to explore who they are becoming, and courageously support them to intentionally leverage their talents and gifts in alignment with their Essence to impact the world.

"Without practices and rituals in place, our fears suck us back into our comfort zone, robbing us of what our soul desires."

Lori Raggio

inspiregreatnesscoaching.com

Chapter 8

If You Don't Go, You Don't Know

Robin Finney

Anticipation consumed me as I organized materials for my upcoming adventure to New Zealand. I had purchased a new rolling duffle bag, backpack for my camera gear, new hiking boots for the mountains I'd climb, and a new fleece to keep me warm. As I placed my passport next to the gear, my heart filled with great wonder and anticipation. It was August of 2014, and THIS was the trip that would change my life, or so I thought. I was nearing the end of my 20s, bored with life, and dreaming of starting a new life.

I was working a corporate marketing job at the time and remember asking my boss if I could take three weeks off to go on this adventure with my two best travel buddies. I had never asked for this much time off at once. I had prepared a whole speech to enroll her in saying "yes." I used to carry so much anxiety around asking. To my surprise, she said "yes." I kind of felt like Cinderella - if I could complete all my tasks in advance, I could go to the Ball.

I can still smell the crisp cool air as I think back to arriving in Dunedin, New Zealand. We had landed in the South Island where it was nearing winter. My heart immediately filled with great awe. I didn't dare to tell my friends, but I had high hopes that maybe THIS would be the trip where I didn't return home; maybe

I'd meet someone; or maybe I'd find my purpose and know what I wanted in life. One thing I knew, I didn't want to go back to my life in the States. I was hungering for more. As such, I placed great attachment to this experience changing my life for the better.

My time in New Zealand was epic. It was an adventure at every turn with stunning views, hikes, bungee jumping, and skydiving. As the trip came to an end, I remember standing in the parking lot of the rental car agency and seeing the most beautiful double rainbow in the sky. Rainbows are a sign of promise. I had this feeling that I would return one day. That even though I didn't find what I was looking for this time around, *one day* I would be living my dream and traveling the world. One day I would finally know what my purpose is.

I returned to the States and entered a deep depression. It was common for me to go through a mini post-vacation depression upon returning from trips. But this time, it felt darker. I felt like my hopes had been extinguished. I felt like I would continue to be trapped and that nothing would change in my life.

I felt hopeless.

When I turned 30, I decided enough was enough. I needed support. I was tired of feeling like my life was going nowhere. I was tired of living the same routine. I was tired of not taking chances.

I sought counseling, enrolled in a seminar about living a life of velocity, and began doing inner work. It would still take years to get to where I wanted to be, but this was the first step.

Showing up for myself and taking the steps to receive

support transformed my life. It made such a difference to know that I was not alone in my struggle. It made a difference to have other people hold space for me and my own healing and transformation.

In August of 2015 (a year after I traveled to New Zealand), I was getting ready for my first photo shoot. Ever since I was a child, I dreamed of modeling in a photo shoot in an abandoned warehouse. I envisioned wearing a beautiful outfit and being in the spotlight. A friend of mine who is a photographer was offering a Celebration Photo Shoot. I lit up when I saw her offer and booked. I went shopping and found the perfect outfits to wear. We met at an abandoned warehouse in downtown Dallas. My vision was coming to life! Prior to the photo shoot, we had an exploratory call to set intentions for the photo shoot. She asked me to choose three words that I wanted to embody during my photo shoot. I chose the words Beauty, Freedom, and Fun.

The photo shoot captured my intentions so powerfully. When I saw the photos, I was stunned by their beauty. And it wasn't just the photos...for the first time in my life, I felt beautiful on the inside and outside.

This photo shoot transformed my view of myself and my life. 2015 was the year that kickstarted my transformation and living a life of intention. I continued participating in transformational workshops and seminars.

In 2017, I discovered meditation and became committed to my yoga practice. It was the year that I began trusting that the Universe was supporting me in saying "yes" to investing in myself. I attended my first meditation retreat in Guatemala. On the very first day, we sat in our inner circle to meditate, and I got a clear message that I was playing it safe in life. When the meditation was complete, we shared what showed up for us. I broke down in tears as I felt the weight of my message. I looked at the group and said, *"I am tired of playing it safe."*

To me, playing it safe meant always living with other people so I wouldn't have to commit to being in a lease, staying at the same job for a decade while dreaming of traveling the world, and never dating or taking a chance on love. I lived in great fear of being trapped. I thought that by making plans, getting in a relationship, or finding a new purpose, I would be trapped if it didn't work out. So, I chose to stay safe in my comfort zone. Being in your comfort zone can be a dangerous place to stay in. Dangerous because it's comfortable and you're less likely to make changes.

My job pays well. I don't love it, but it pays well. Why should I risk giving up a steady paycheck? My relationship isn't exciting anymore. He's all I've ever known though. What if I leave him and I don't find anyone else? What if I ask someone to be my client and they say no? What if I don't get any clients, and I have to go back to working for someone else? What if I leave and it all falls through? What if I'm stuck with no job, no home, and must start all over again?

Yet, if we don't try, we'll never know. If we don't go, we don't know. *"If I don't go, I don't know."* That became my motto. At the end of the retreat in Guatemala, I got clear that it was time to get out of my comfort zone, turn in my notice, and follow my dream of traveling the world. I knew that if I didn't dive all in, and go for it, I would continue to create excuses and reasons why I couldn't leave. I knew that the longer I stayed, the harder it would be to leave and to trust that the Universe had my back.

In May of 2018, I said goodbye to my company, career, and colleagues of 11 years. I sold my furniture and most of my belongings and turned in the keys to my apartment after only three and a half months of living there. I said goodbye to a steady paycheck, a life of security and comfort, and set off on a one-way flight to Australia. I spent my first week in Australia basking in the astonishment of quitting my job, leaving the United States, and becoming a nomad. It felt surreal as I stood on the balcony of the Park Hyatt with champagne in hand, watching the sun set over the Sydney Opera House.

My life felt like a dream.

I spent the next eight months only buying one-way tickets and trusting my intuition to guide me where to go. After spending six weeks in Thailand, I was clear that I was living my dream. I just didn't know how to sustain it. When I quit my job, I left with one month's pay, my quarterly bonus, and about $500 in savings. I wasn't ready to look for a new job or start anything on my own - I literally wanted to buy myself more time. I had plans to be back in the States for an event, and knew the next best option would be to sell my car.

After selling my car, I decided to head to Mexico. A friend of mine had recommended visiting San Miguel de Allende. When I Googled the city, I was immediately drawn in by its ornate buildings and vibrant colors. I was inspired and knew I wanted to do a photo shoot.

I found an eye-catching red lace romper, packed my heels, and headed to Mexico. I hired a local photographer through some connections and scheduled my photo shoot. On the day of my photo shoot, I decided to treat myself to a manicure and pedicure. As I was paying for my services, the owner asked me what I was doing while visiting San Miguel. I told him that I had a photo shoot scheduled for that afternoon. His eyes immediately lit up. He looked at me and exclaimed, "Oh! You must come back here before your photo shoot and let me do your makeup!"

My makeup? Did I need professional makeup? I was getting professional photos taken, after all, so why not? I agreed and came back that afternoon. I was so present to the joy that Manuel, my stylist, expressed as he used his talents to make me over. I saw the same joy on the photographer's face as he took me to his favorite places in his city. Both men were so honored that I, a foreigner, would come to their country and allow them to share their gifts with me.

This experience changed my life and opened a doorway to my mission of modeling in photo shoots in countries all over the world to support local photographers, designers, artists, and stylists.

It all started because I chose to follow my heart and trust my intuition to guide me. Since that day in Mexico, I've modeled in 11 photo shoots (eight international and three domestic). The whole mission has been an incredible experience of trust, surrender, and allowing life to lead the way. I'm amazed every time I show up in a country and watch the magic unfold. Everything is beautifully orchestrated and synchronized from connecting to the photographers and stylists to finding the perfect outfit.

When we are present to reality and believe that each moment, each choice, and each answer is all beautifully orchestrated to create this thing called life, beauty is present in all of it.

Going on this spiritual journey and surrendering to the flow of life - selling my belongings, buying one-way tickets, solo traveling to 19 countries across six continents in the span of 18 months, modeling in photo shoots, and saying "yes" to transformation - has opened my eyes and heart to my intuitive nature and gifts. I've learned to trust that everything is being orchestrated for me. I've gained great patience and have spent years shedding layers and allowing my whole self to be seen.

It all started the moment I looked out and saw the double rainbow in New Zealand and believed life had more in store for me.

If you don't go, you don't know.

Today, I use all of the experiences I've lived to support others in living life to its fullest. I believe at the core of being human, we all have a desire to be seen and heard. Yet, we're often afraid to allow our authentic selves to be seen because it might not be safe. Others may not understand or approve. By learning to own and live who we are and what we want, we give others permission to do the same.

I am grateful to support other women in allowing their authentic selves to be seen through individual and group intuitive clarity sessions, "soul-o" travel retreats, and photo shoot experiences.

About Robin

Robin Finney is an intuitive and authenticity guide, retreat leader, writer, international model and speaker, world traveler, and founder of Wandering Aunt. She supports others in allowing their authentic self to be seen through intuitive clarity sessions, "soulo" travel retreats, and photo shoot experiences.

Robin believes that at the core of being human, we all have a desire to be seen and heard. Robin uses her work as an intuitive guide to create safe spaces for this core desire to be present. Robin lives a bold, unconventional life as a nomad traveling where she is pulled. Since 2018, Robin has traveled solo to 19 countries across six continents and modeled in eight international photo shoots as part of her mission to support local photographers, designers, and artists.

"When we are present to reality and believe that each moment, each choice, and each answer is all beautifully orchestrated to create this thing called life, beauty is present in all of it."

Robin Finney

wanderingaunt.com

Power

unity

victor

resilience

goddess

Chapter 9

You Are Never Alone

Julia Bernadsky

It is 1989, Kiev. The huge communist empire of the Soviet Union is just about to collapse. People are full of uncertainty and fear about the future. It feels even less safe here than ever before.

I am 19. Nine months pregnant. Laying on the couch with contractions.

The doctor said, "Be ready. You could give birth to your baby any time now."

I am ready. No problem. I just need a few more hours, so I get on the plane.

I thought, "As long as I step inside the plane, it's all good, it's no longer Russia. As long as my baby is born on the other side of the iron curtain..."

I am trying to move as little as possible, convincing my body to slow down the labor process, and watching my friends pack my whole life into two suitcases.

The last time I saw my family was six months ago. I remember how devastated my mom was. She was consumed by the fear that she would never see me again. Leaving our home country without me was her greatest pain.

My father had a vision that we will all come to America where we will be free and be able to rebuild our lives, create a real home, and be safe. But the only way this dream could become reality is if they go now, while the doors are still open.

My mom was in a trance. The only thing that she could think about was that she may never see me again.

Before my family left for good, my mom gave me a little gold necklace she created for me and engraved with these words, "I am praying for you, my little daughter. Mama."

All her love, her desire to protect me, to hold me, to be with me and help me, all that she had in her, she, without realizing it, encapsulated into this little gold necklace. From that moment on I would wear this necklace all the time.

Time to go to the airport...

The two suitcases are packed and I don't even know what's in them. We have $250 total. We are ready!

I was very lucky because I didn't look pregnant. I was tall, lean and deliberately wearing a mini skirt with a large tunic over it. Nobody could even suspect that I was pregnant! That was my ticket to get on the plane.

Little did they know I was having contractions... I was asking my baby to please wait just a little bit longer... I was holding the necklace my mom gave me and saying to myself, "Go without the fear, go without the fear, everything will be ok."

Finally, we arrived in Vienna. It was a miracle. My son Boris was born on September 4th, 1989 in Vienna's most beautiful hospital.

My son was born in the FREE WORLD!!!

In my eyes, everything was perfect. Not easy, but a truly incredible journey.

I have no idea how I understood what doctors were saying when I was giving birth-they spoke German and I didn't. Later on I had so many questions about how to care for my baby, and because of the language barrier, had nobody to explain it to me. But, somehow, I knew that everything was going to be OK.

Using the last few cents we had, my husband was able to make a very short phone call to my family in New York City, to tell them that Boris was born, we were safe in Vienna, and everything is good.

This was only the beginning of my journey. Ahead we had lots more to go through until we finally reached America.

Maybe it was my mama's prayers, her energy, and her huge love that helped us to get through it all. I will not know for sure. But I do know that I was never alone and somehow my angels were with me every step of the way.

The necklace my mom made for me became my amulet. This piece allowed me to connect and embody the energy needed to go through this journey.

It held that unconditional love that is stronger than any tests and challenges in life.

It helped me to trust myself when I needed to learn quickly how to take care of my brand new little person.

It helped me to learn how to be vulnerable and at the same time to have courage and strength at the moments I needed the most.

Isn't it fascinating how objects can seed a powerful feeling of energy and love?

What I want to leave you with is this: Every object around us is energy.

Go find your amulet, YOUR piece that holds and helps you elevate YOUR energy vibration, supports you on your life's journey, helps you align with who you really are, makes you feel LOVED and reminds you that YOU ARE NEVER ALONE.

With love,

Julia

P.S.- At first, when I looked back at this story I thought, "I did it!" I did everything humanly possible, and beyond, and that is why we were able to get out of the big jail we lived in, and that is why my son was born in the free world. But now I know that it wasn't just me...we were protected and guided every moment of the way.

P.P.S.- The necklace my mama gave me planted seeds for Untamed Hearts, the brand I created 27 years later. Untamed Hearts is a purpose driven brand where we create beautiful & meaningful jewelry / objects infused with energy of unconditional love and protection. Each piece in our collection has a unique story to tell. In your hands, with your intention, it becomes your amulet and helps you call forth higher vibration of energy, empowers you on your life journey, inspires you to open your heart, heal, and embrace our differences. Our pieces are stamped with "Peace For All" - it's our message to the world. Everything made by Untamed Hearts is Vegan and 100% Cruelty Free.

About Julia

Julia Bernadsky is an entrepreneur, artist, designer and the creator of Untamed Hearts. She works with energy, guided by highly attuned intuitions, and is also a Theta Healer.

All parts of her work come together through Untamed Hearts, a purpose-driven brand where she creates beautiful and meaningful objects / jewelry infused with energy. Each piece in the collection has a story to tell. In your hands it becomes an amulet that helps raise your energy vibration, empowers you on your life journey, inspires you to open your heart, heal, and embrace our differences. All pieces are stamped with "Peace For All" - their message to the world.

Born in the soulful city Kiev (Ukraine), Julia came to New York City in 1989 with big dreams and a lot of passion for life. She feels fortunate to have had a pretty cool career in fashion, as well as holding a glamorous position at high-end brands as a creative director in digital product and experience design. Julia often says, "My work is all about bridging the realms of energy, beauty, consciousness and healing. My passion is to inspire people to live a powerful and intentional life that is aligned with their truth."

"Find YOUR piece that makes you powerful beyond measure, that makes you feel LOVED, and reminds you that you are never alone."

Julia Bernadsky

untamedhearts.com

Chapter 10

The Victor All Along

Jacqueline A. Baldwin

After 25 years of marriage, two living children, and three unborn children in heaven, it all comes down to this. A briskly-stark and cold December day in 2017, I am waiting in the dingy and confining five by five conference room in the heavy courthouse for judgment to be laid down with the gavel, before turning to the next case. To the judge, we are just another statistical couple on the docket for the day making the decision to uncouple. But for me, this was a day that would drastically change the trajectory of my life forever.

I can see him in the hallway through the small window in the door in an otherwise windowless room. I felt like a bird in a bush. Somewhat protected as long as I can remain undiscovered. There was nothing preventing the door from being opened, and then I would have nowhere to run and hide. There was only one way in and out!

My breath shortened and quickened as if I were running a race. I could hear my heart beating as blood rushed to my head. A whirlwind of all sorts of memories flew past my eyes as if I were pressing the fast forward button on a movie so I could see how it would end.

There was the memory of when we first met. So handsome, intensely engaging. My eyes began to fill with water. *Was I making a mistake? It wasn't ALL bad!*

Then came the flashes of the not so "good" parts! The suffocating control through hidden, mismanaged finances, reckless decisions in family planning, perpetual gaslighting, the unpredictable moments of rage followed by flowers all keeping me off center and creating insufferable self-doubt. My third unwanted abortion, this one following the birth of our second child, left me broken beyond repair (or so I thought). I was immersed with haunting self-doubt, shame, and loathing. It must have been that it was ME. *Was I an unfit mother? Was I an insufficient life partner?* The deep trauma throughout these two and half decades would at times pull me under the water nearly drowning me.

Then the images graciously ceased and I was again focused on the here and now. I was sure I was going to pass out or throw up while I waited for my attorney to come back from negotiating the final agreement. I felt helpless, alone, DEFEATED. The horrifying images then resumed relentlessly. This time, they flipped back to the 4-year-old girl who was made to feel dirty by her grandfather. I immediately felt like that helpless, confused, frightened little girl who retreated to a place of fearful solitude.

Then it hit me at that moment like a sledgehammer. In reality, my entire 47 years of life since that time had been spent living in a metaphorical small, dingy five-foot square room with a tiny window in the one door just like the one I found myself actually sitting in. The small window gave glimpses of what was just beyond the door. Most of what I could see in snippets was terrifying to me.

Once in a while, I would see glimpses of a kind but unrecognizable face peek in at me through the window, inviting me in a muffled voice to step out through the door. But most of the time I saw an imposing figure I came to know as Control. He was looming over me making me feel small and insignificant. When I did leave the room, it was in the company of Control and his compatriots, Self-Doubt and Rejection. They were always guarding the door of my self-imposed prison. Sometimes, all three would escort me through the narrow halls of my life. As we made our way down through the confining walls, it seemed to me Control always kept a firm grip on my arm, squeezing and pulling me close if I veered down an intersecting hall where I could hear my name being called, oh, so faintly. I could never quite make out who it was that knew my name and called ever so sweetly. That all changed on one fateful day.

While my transition to freedom from that self-imposed prison began years before, my transformation began in earnest at that courthouse on that December day.

On August 19, 2016, while Control, Self-Doubt, and Rejection must have briefly left the door unattended, Redeemer snuck in, hushing me as to not bring attention. "Quickly," he said, "I have something to show you." Images from a lifetime of deceit, lies, and covert ops emblazoned in my mind, blinding yet so clear. Images of tremendous authentic love followed a suit of armor for protection and the faintest image of freedom awaited me.

Redeemer gave me a light kiss on my cheek, whispering to take heart, knowing he and others would be just outside the door when I was ready to step out. He then left as quietly and quickly as he came. My head was spinning, heart racing, as I began the nearly two-year emotional rollercoaster that would render me terrified, exhilarated, let down, raised up, and nearly broken all at the same time.

The images that Redeemer had shown me, replayed over and

over again. I felt betrayed, gullible, rejected, full of regret and shame. Yet, at the same time a glimmer of a refreshing emotion crept in, emboldening me. That was a completely new emotion for me. That was the armor I had seen in the images. I began to slowly pick up pieces and try them on. They seemed a bit uncomfortable at first, heavy and rigid. Was this armor really meant for me or was it left behind by someone who no longer needed it? But as I continued to wear it, adding more and more pieces, I came to realize that it was made to fit me perfectly. I began to feel safe to venture out through the door and explore what lay beyond.

Greeting total strangers, no longer fearing if they meant to cause me harm, I grew confident in my newfound fortitude. I took time on these journeys to stop and reflect, daring to revisit those dark recesses in my memories and cast light on them so the fear they used to engender no longer held me captive. I came to know that I was NOT DEFEATED, but rather I had survived. In fact, I had more than survived! I had been the VICTOR all along. Being able to go back to each moment in my life, when I thought I was weak and beaten, and to see the strength I had instead allowed me to celebrate these life experiences rather than bemoan them.

After the longest roller coaster ride ever, the final straightaway came and the car pulled into the station. I got off, drained, hair blown to bits, but standing ready to jump back on when a new car comes around. I now know that life will be a constant roller coaster. Thrilling, at times terrifying, and other times just gliding along on the straight stretches of track where you can catch your breath before the next unexpected twist or drop. I have learned to embrace the entire ride, to lean into the turns with my hands up in the air screaming with reckless abandon. No longer am I intimidated by the steepest drops.

Bring them on! I know I am held safe throughout. It may get bumpy along the way, but that brings contrast and appreciation to the smooth moments.

I also decided to vacate the dingy five by five room, slamming the door with the small window as I left Control, Self-Doubt, and Rejection behind in total bewilderment as to where I had gone.

Today, I look in the mirror and see an entirely transformed woman standing before me. I almost don't recognize myself as I continue to evolve daily. I harken back to the days when my sons were babies. During their first year of life, when I would put them to bed at night and then pick them up from their crib in the morning, I swore they looked different literally overnight. Their facial expressions became more animated each day as they were drinking up all new life experiences as if through a firehose.

My transformation has been as dramatic, especially in these last eight months. I used to look at others and see the ease with which they moved, and I wondered what that actually was and how it must feel. I had always moved with trepidation and fear as if in fight-or-flight 24/7. This took its toll on me emotionally and physically. I had all but given up hope that I would truly ever know what it would be like not to be ridden with worry. At long last, through unwavering determination, gut wrenching self-discovery, and deepening faith, I have been able to heal and attain the ease and peace I had so desperately been seeking.

I do not look back on my life with any regret. The experiences I have had, good, bad and ugly, are all part of who I am. They have tempered me. I now stand strong, confident, and lovingly powerful. I embrace my beautiful imperfect self, scars and all. I choose to see my scars not as wounds that did not heal completely, but rather as a reminder of the victories I have won.

Just as the scars that remain from the many surgeries I have had provide markers in time when my body was in disrepair, so the emotional scars provide markers for how far I have come on my own transformation journey. They are also humbling reminders for me to have compassion for my brothers and sisters who undoubtedly have their own wounds that require healing.

My mission now is to offer a beautifully scarred and loving hand to those who are just beginning to peek out the door of their own five by five room. I want to share the message of hope that Redeemer shared with me on that fateful day in August. There is so much beauty, joy, and peace awaiting you. Only YOU can choose to take that first bold step out the door. Redeemer, Love, and Support are waiting to come alongside you. To lift you if you stumble, to comfort you if you are afraid, to help you stand up undaunted to Control, Self-Doubt, and Rejection.

You see, my suit of armor, meant for protection in those earlier days, has been transformed into more of a superhero suit revealing my extraordinary "super power." I have been uniquely honed to be a guide for women seeking freedom from their five by five room. I am standing just outside the door ready to walk, holding their hand as they discover how to boldly and conspicuously walk in their own transformation. I want them to feel the same peace and joy I feel today.

About Jackie

Jacqueline A. Baldwin is passionate about eradicating financial vulnerability. Her specialty is advising women who feel financially unprepared for the big what-ifs in life so they can feel confident knowing they have solutions for weathering any kind of storm. Jackie felt financially vulnerable throughout her former marriage and vowed that she never wanted to feel that level of vulnerability again. From this experience, her desire to help others to feel safe, secure, and enlightened was born. Great confidence comes from knowing that with the right guidance you can not only survive the great what-ifs in life that come your way, including economic challenges, but you *can* also thrive and experience a vibrant future.

"I choose to see my scars not as wounds that did not heal completely but rather as reminders of the victories I have won."

Jacqueline A. Baldwin

blfinarc.com

Chapter 11

Mascara & Muay Thai

Gina Marecki

Blackest noir mascara and lip gloss with names like Strawberry Fizz, Berry Flash, and Grapefruit Blast boost my confidence to take on the world or my group exercise class feeling wide-eyed, smiling, and ready. Squeeze tubes of glittery pink can be found stashed in my car, handbag, gym bag, coat pocket, and probably several other places that I forget.

No one would know that this was my mask, hiding my past. During my 30s, I'd been fighting effects of past trauma, including depression, sudden panic attacks, flashbacks, and insomnia. Fitness was my way out of the darkness, helping me overcome the mental obstacles that prevented me from fully loving myself.

Instead of a dismal gray outlook, I opted for Strawberry Fizz, a sparkly pink shade of lipgloss. The blackest noir mascara reflected the depression that lurked beneath the surface and brought out a spark that was yearning to be set free.

The darkness and gloom of depression and anxiety took over, despite my appearance of a perfect life. Depression is something that cannot be controlled or ignored no matter how many times I told myself to "get over it" or tried to fight it. It forced its way to the surface, despite how much I tried to cover it. Covering it was like trying to pour a concrete foundation over a wave pool.

There were days I didn't feel anything. I was numb.

Thoughts of driving off the side of the road, ending it all, sounded appealing. I fought on, determined to win this battle and be there for my family. It was difficult to keep up the façade of a happy wife, mother, daughter, friend, member of society as the darkness settled over me, dragging me down. I fought silently to get through each day with a smile as I became filled with rage, anxiety, anger, and pain, like a volcano ready to erupt. I was thankful for the support of a compassionate husband and the unconditional love of my three children, who at the time were aged eight, six, and three. I prayed, went to church, kept faith that I could heal.

I found a refuge from the pain at age 38 when I sought out a behavioral therapist. We worked through the roots of my depression and anxiety starting with childhood trauma, an unhealthy lifestyle, and a physically abusive relationship in my 20s.

By adding anti-depressants and anti-anxiety medications, life became steady, predictable, and that was good. I became happy in my safety net.

Then, a spark was lit when I began to exercise. A feeling that brought me back to the land of the living. I began to experience emotions, feelings, things that had lay dormant.

Adding exercise to my life changed my outlook from bleak to vibrant by filling me with a rush of feel-good hormones each day. While the antidepressants helped tremendously for two and a half years, my goal was to cease taking them. When I stopped taking the medicine, there was a moment of doubt, but I quickly found that daily movement replaced the need for medication. I added everything from weightlifting, running, tennis, and high intensity training to my days. The more intense the movement, the better I felt.

This transformation in my mood and my entire being propelled me forward to a career as a personal trainer and fitness instructor at age 42. Lip gloss on, waterproof mascara carefully applied, and hair pulled into a ponytail became my pre-game ritual. No matter what loomed under the surface, I was ready to face the day.

My unspoken mission began to unfold. My goal became to help women like me see the beauty and strength that resides deep within all of us, if only we would let each other see behind our masks. I wanted to share that with other women that silently battled the same affliction as I.

As years went on, my depression stayed at bay, but I was burdened with chronic pain and stress partly from overtraining, and partly from hidden trauma. I was sidelined from progressing in my personal and professional fitness journey, and open to trying any possible naturalistic path for a solution: physical therapy, massage, and endless corrective exercises, to no avail. I encountered a trainer specializing in pain management with a neurological based training program. He also happened to be a Muay Thai kickbox instructor. Loving all things strength, cardio, and high intensity related, I was intrigued.

Prior to that time, kickboxing had been my favorite non-contact cardio class at the gym, giving me a feeling of empowerment. Muay Thai kickboxing differs in that it is a contact, combat martial art, referred to as the "Art of Eight Limbs," in which your hands, elbows, legs, and knees are your weapons.

At 46-years-old, I awkwardly learned to move my body in ways I never had, at times wishing I'd learned this skill set earlier in life. Muay Thai challenged me to move far out of my comfort zone.

From the first moment I punched and kicked pads with my trainer, I was hooked. Between kickboxing and a newly acquired neuro-based training program, that chronic pain I mentioned didn't exist, and my stress levels dropped immensely. I would later learn that past trauma to the body can be released with bodywork such as kickboxing, heavy weight training, and targeting specific parts of the nervous system to calm the fight-or-flight response.

Slowly and tentatively, I trained in Muay Thai kickboxing on the mat, a boxing ring, and in a Mixed Martial Arts fight cage, which is an octagon-shaped ring framed with caged walls where fighters compete against each other.

An important part of the kickboxing curriculum is to spar with partners. The idea of being hit by men (and women) wasn't what I had in mind for fun. I loved all other aspects of this sport, so I continued working one-on-one with my trainer who patiently helped me improve.

After several months, my anxiety with sparring didn't lessen. However, I was determined. The first time my trainer swept my legs out from under me, I was shocked. I wasn't sure how to react.

For a moment on the floor of the ring, I was slammed back in time to my 20s, to my apartment in Newton, Massachusetts, where I was arguing with my former boyfriend. He was filled with rage and punched a hole in the wall. I told him he needed to leave and, within seconds, he grabbed my shoulder, swept my legs out from under me, landing me on my kitchen floor. I lay there stunned, then scrambled to stand, determined to fight back. I was met with another sweep of my legs landing me even harder onto the floor. I heard a thump and crying. *Was that me crying?* It should be me because I banged my head hard, and this was my boyfriend who had done this to me. I was numb as I stared at the back door of my apartment, contemplating: *fight or flight?* Then, I chose to run.

Back in the ring, I stood up, unsure of how to respond. My past traumas had left a definitive mark on my psyche, putting my fight-or-flight response on high alert but I forged ahead.

Working through the curriculum of Muay Thai was extremely humbling. I learned a lot about myself, tested through five levels, two of the levels extremely difficult with two-hour group tests where sparring was a large focus. I dedicated hours of my time to improve, riding a roller coaster of emotions as I signed up to test. Then anxiety caused me to pull out. Months later, I finally found the courage to test again, then was pulled aside by the head instructor who said he didn't think I was ready. I needed to improve my sparring. Higher level, higher expectations.

Several months later, despite a rotator cuff tear, self-doubt, and anxiety, my determination was reborn. I dedicated blood, sweat, and tears to my training, waterproof mascara continuing to mask the many tears.

The day of the test, I was armed with my lipgloss, ponytail in, and waterproof mascara on. I dressed in my black satin Muay Thai fight shorts with pink trim, iridescent purple Fairtek boxing gloves, black Fighter shin guards, and pink mouth guard. Now age 48, I tentatively lined up on the mat with the 19 other testers, most of whom were in their 20s and 30s. Five of us were testing for the advanced level, four guys and me.

I endured two hours of grueling pad-work, intense cardio, and sparring. The five of us sparring at this higher level were encircled by the other participants, instructors, and family members. The two male instructors could pull us aside to spar at any time in this sparring circle. The ultimate dance off.

I fought through four two-minute rounds with different partners, one punch glancing my face, fending off a bloody nose. There was one round left. *Who would I be paired with?* I kept my eyes down, avoiding eye contact with the head Muay Thai instructor. He was skilled and fast. He made it known that he'd failed his own children in testing. *Don't look at him, I told myself, maybe he'll forget about me.*

The buzzer rang and he called my name. Everything moved at lightning speed. I moved to avoid his strikes and block his kicks. This was the test right here, all or nothing. Caught in a clinch, when the opponent grabs your head and holds you in, trying to render you helpless, you respond.I quickly remembered how to free myself. Then I felt it.

Feeling the warmth flowing down my face, the nudge of his shoulder brought on my bloody nose. I touched my glove to my face. A red smudge colored the white trim of my sparkling purple boxing glove. I thought I could stop the test, grab a tissue, get some sympathy, maybe run...no such luck. My instructor encouraged me to keep going.

"You can do this," he said, "You look badass." Somehow, I dug deep and found that inner strength to once again forge on. Striking where I could as I held one arm up to my face, smearing the blood like war paint. A fighter, a warrior.

For a second, I thought, *what the heck am I doing?* But I didn't have time to dwell on that as his punches and kicks knocked those thoughts away. I just needed to fight.

When the final buzzer rang, my instructor gave me a hug announcing that he'd been saving himself up to spar with me. A girl from class handed me a box of tissues while my male sparring partners tapped me on the shoulder and patted me on the head with their gloves saying nice job. I held tissues to my nose and they avoided stepping in the blood spatter across the mats.

I was fine, nothing broken, no cuts or abrasions, just a bloody nose. I was so exhausted I don't even think my ego was bruised.

All I knew was I finished. I completed something that I never thought I'd be able to accomplish.

I stood posing for a picture holding my certificate, by myself, legs and hands shaking proudly, humbly, and confirming what I knew about myself.

I am a survivor.

I am a fighter.

I am resilient.

About Gina

Gina Marecki pursued her passion for fitness by becoming a certified personal trainer and women's fitness specialist in 2012. After four years she expanded her business and opened G Fitness studio in Simsbury, Connecticut, where she added barre, nutrition, and corporate wellness for female-based companies. Her clients include regular fitness enthusiasts, athletes, and those who have suffered past injuries, depression, trauma, autoimmune diseases, and cancer. She uses her kickboxing experience to help women feel empowered. Her marketing background has helped her to promote and grow her business.

Gina began creative writing when faced with depression and recently participated in writer's workshops with the goal of publishing a work of fiction. Gina resides in Simsbury with her husband, Vaughan, of 22 years. They have three children and two cats.

"My unspoken mission began to unfold. My goal became to help women like me see the beauty and strength that resides deep within all of us, if only we would let each other see behind our masks."

Gina Marecki

gfitness.us

Chapter 12

Hot Mess to Goddess

Kacey Cardin, PCC

I was born a too loud girl in a too small town. My parents divorced soon after I was born, and I let my dad's departure serve as evidence that I wasn't worth sticking around for. After an assault in high school left me so traumatized that I temporarily lost my memory of it, I spent my 20s searching for love that I was convinced I didn't deserve. I looked for it in bottles and in the beds of strangers. I cut myself down, and, in my darkest moments, I cut myself open. Feeling broken was sometimes better than feeling nothing at all.

The day I turned 30, I got fired from my New York City "survival job," became a professional dominatrix, and resolved to hire a life coach once I'd whipped and teased my way to enough money to cover her $3,000 fee. I never could have imagined that would turn into a career pivot, a spiritual awakening, and a self-love breakthrough that would create the first healthy relationship of my life and a six-figure coaching business of my own. 2020 prompted me to revisit my hometown and its role as a catalyst for transformation in my life. I hope my story helps you uncover more of your own.

As a child, I was a mini boss: creative, assertive, bold - a leader of the pack. I wasn't always the most empathetic little leader, though. Little girls my age learned early on that there was only room at the table for one of us, and I was hungry enough to chew up any other girl who tried to steal my spot. I was desperate to be loved, and my insatiable appetite for acceptance turned into a desperate hunger for control.

In 7th grade, that hunger bit me in the butt when the "I Hate Kacey" Club was formed. Is there any living creature more vicious than a 7th grade girl? We were all just trying to find our way, but bullying, rejection, and social isolation cut deep and reawakened the fear that I wasn't worthy of being loved. Seeing that my smarts and high spiritedness had taken me from mini boss to outcast overnight, I chose to fixate on my body as the key to love and acceptance.

As a teenager, I felt so alive when I was enjoying or punishing my body that it didn't matter anymore if girls at school liked me or if I was finally "good enough" to escape the harsh criticism of an overprotective parent. When my body got compliments, especially from boys, I felt valuable and worthy of love and respect. My body held my pride and vanity. I was active and energetic, and I loved feeling strong; my body was muscular, and I thought that was beautiful. My body also held onto my rage and shame for me. It was resilient enough to withstand the razors and knives that I used to slice into my inner forearms when I needed a physical wound to help me make sense of the invisible, emotional pain I felt. Self-destruction is not the fast or easy route to self-love, but I was never one to do things the easy way.

My distrust of others' loyalty meant that I had commitment issues of my own. Even in grade school, I'd secretly "go with" two boyfriends at the same time or kiss a boy on a school trip while my boyfriend sat a few rows ahead on the bus, finding himself the subject of ridicule while I sat, proud for not letting anyone have my heart, blind to how his little heart was hurt by my antics. I was so sure that I didn't matter; it was hard to believe my actions had any bearing on another person's feelings.

By 16, my self-image relied heavily on outside approval, so two weeks before school started, when my friend Chris - quarterback, star student, handsome, and one of many ex-boyfriends - invited me over to watch a movie one afternoon, I hoped he still found me attractive. If he liked me, others would like me, and popularity seemed like the cure for everything at 16.

Things did not go as planned. That day was a blur. Three weeks into the school year, Chris wouldn't talk to me, the old IHK Club was starting rumors, and I started having debilitating panic attacks and seizures nearly every day. I lost interest in my schoolwork. I had trouble remembering things - car keys, homework assignments, huge chunks of time each week. Predictably, the seizures did not increase my popularity or level of self-acceptance, and despite a cocktail of Prozac and anti-seizure meds, depression and anxiety became my closest companions. I wanted to disappear into myself until I could get the hell out of that town. Surely my fears and failures wouldn't follow me.

The body holds on to what the mind can't process, though, so I unwittingly packed up my emotional baggage and took it with me to Vanderbilt. Despite ongoing depression, anxiety, and ADHD, college was a reawakening of mind and spirit for me. The more I rediscovered my authentic self, the less often I had seizures. Clearly, there was a link between my emotions and the seizures, but surely 7th grade bullying or my parents' divorce wouldn't still be causing such turmoil...

My mind finally revealed its secrets to me one night at a Sexual Assault Awareness seminar. Right there on the floor of the Tri Delt house, tears silently streaming down my red hot face, I was back in my hometown on Chris' couch two weeks before junior year. Repressed memories flooded back like movie scenes, including the one of Chris pinning me down on his couch. Shock and shame set in as my mind registered what my body had been trying to tell me all those years. My body remembered, but my brain had to forget.

It all came back to me: Chris asking if I still liked him "like that" as he brushed a stray curl from my face and leaned in close before shoving me backward. With the repulsive feeling of his sweat dripping onto my face and mixing with my tears, I hadn't realized I was crying until the salty mixture rolled down my cheeks. I felt the sensation of simultaneously being trapped on that couch but also standing outside looking in through the window, unable to save myself from what was about to happen.

The sound of him unzipping my pants with one hand while his other hand stayed on my neck. His hot, wretched breath on my face as he worked two fingers into me, despite my tears and pleas for him to stop. My voice begging, "Please stop! Please don't do this. We don't want to do this. I don't want this. You don't want to do this. Please. No no no no. Please. Stop."

His smile as he forced himself into my rigid body. My fear that it might never end, even though it must only have been a few minutes. He was so turned on by the conquest that he could barely contain himself, despite the tears and snot on my face. How I froze. How my body and I betrayed each other in that moment.

The sound of the cushion springs squeaking with every piercing thrust that broke a little more of my spirit and stole a little more of my light. His weight on top of me, stealing my breath as he stole consent to my body and to an act that, up until then, I had associated with pleasure and freedom. Wishing I could sink my fingernails into his eyeballs, then immediately feeling guilty for wanting to hurt him, and not being able to move my arms anyway. The level of fight I held onto until my body went limp with defeat as he went limp with release.

Watching him wipe off his crotch with a white T-shirt. My stiff, awkward movements, like a mannequin trying to pull up my pants and adjust my halter top, wondering if this all happened because I hadn't worn a bra that day. My hands shaking as I reached for my purse as he sat, stunned, on the couch, and said, "Wow. You really didn't want to do that, did you?"

"No, Chris. I didn't. And you did it anyway."

Walking out the front door. Getting back into my little red pick-up truck. Listening to *Torn* on repeat all the way back home but not hearing a single note of it. Feeling his semen pour out of my vagina. Wishing I could cut myself in half so I'd never feel that sensation again.

My seizures gradually stopped altogether as I worked through the traumatic memories of literally being held down by someone I had trusted and the shame that comes from not being able to protect someone you love from harm.

Remembering the assault was a catalyst for me to reintroduce my body, mind, and soul to one another, but it took time to build trust within myself. I finished college, had two stable relationships, got a master's degree, and found my healing journey exponentially catapulted by a summer arts program in LA that introduced me to a routine of daily yoga, dance therapy, journaling, and singing on stage without inviting my inner critic to join me. When I moved to New York City in 2009, I was healthier than ever and ready to conquer the world. I'd found my soul again.

Beliefs that take hold during trauma are insidious, though. They operate quietly in the background, slowly re-infecting even the healthiest, strongest parts of your psyche.

My first few years in New York City were magical. I landed my first agent, helped launch a burlesque troupe, toured Europe with a show I co-wrote, appeared on stage and screen, auditioned at the Metropolitan Opera, and rediscovered the joy of feeling safe in my own body again through the art of burlesque and the deepening of my yoga practice. In spite of evidence that I was loved and respected, though, I was plagued deep down with a story that I was human garbage, meant to be used then tossed aside. No amount of professional accolades or great first dates were convincing me otherwise. I continued to use sex as a weapon, sometimes against other people and sometimes against myself. Sex felt exciting, powerful, vital. Love felt either perilous or boring. I would practice yoga by day and binge drinking by night. Life became a bohemian, bipolar, ambitious attempt to outrun the shadows of abandonment and assault.

Our comfort zone works like a rubber band. The first few times you stretch it, it'll snap back on you hard and fast, and then feel smaller than it did before you stretched it. If you stretch it out a few more times - perhaps more slowly at first - before you know it, that band can hold far more than you ever thought possible. The year I turned 30, my rubber band snapped back hard enough to literally knock me out. New York City had been about bliss, purpose, and adventure, then I got scared of my own immense possibility, so my defense mechanisms kicked in and kept me safe by having me pack on a few pounds, bomb a slew of auditions, and meet up with an abusive ex who got drunk at brunch and punched me so hard that he knocked me out cold right in the middle of Bedford Avenue. The next month, I got fired, leaving me with $250 in the bank the day rent was due.

What was a sexually-empowered actor and former mini-boss to do? Five days later, I was in a shady one-person elevator in a midtown Manhattan office building, a whip in my purse and a smile in my heart, on my way to day one as a professional dominatrix. I didn't last long on the job. I knew that if I didn't handle my own internal conflict around love, sex, and spirituality, I wasn't much better off than the guy paying hundreds of dollars to have a strange woman beat him with a whip while he licked her shoes.

A friend had encouraged me a year earlier to meet her life coach. "Sounds like a made up job," I'd snorted into my mimosa. As usual, I didn't do things the fast or easy way, but finally, I hired her. Six months later, I was in coach training myself. It was in that training that I finally understood the difference between responsibility and blame. I released my shameful anger and found a sacred rage that mobilized a profound inner transformation. I learned the power of forgiveness, and I met my soul level self. I realized that power isn't the key to love, but that self-love is the key to true power.

One week after graduation, I treated myself to a solo vacation in Key West. A night of dancing turned into a late night sailboat makeout with a handsome stranger who put me in a chokehold and unzipped his pants. For a split second, my fear and my soul waged war: *Was I worthless or was I divine? Was I going to endure another assault?* My sacred rage awoke, and for the first time in my life, I fought for myself from a deep sense of self-worth and love. He stopped, sputtering that he didn't know what had come over him. It didn't matter. All that mattered was that I had my power back, no matter what life threw at me, because I had love and power within. All those years spent looking for it in other people or their approval. It was with me all along, waiting for me to fully accept myself and allow the integration of my body, mind, and soul.

In 2019, on a beach in Costa Rica while leading a Divinely Expressed Women's retreat, I looked back on all of these events. It really hit me then that I had transformed "from hot mess to goddess" by leaning deeply into the discomfort of trusting myself and my spirit. Now, in 2020, I'm grateful that my journey has me well-equipped to support others on theirs. Love is not about picking and choosing the parts of you or others that are "acceptable." It's about learning to love all the parts of who you are, and life is the toughest teacher you'll ever have. You *are* constant transformation.

Being human is an innately traumatic experience for a soul. We're bombarded with experiences and relationships that test the integrity of our body+mind+soul connection. None of us make it through life without a breakdown that leads us to stray from that wholeness. Transformation is what occurs when we find our way back to it.

About Kacey

Kacey Cardin, ACCC, PCC, is a dynamic executive and leadership coach, facilitator, and trainer whose work has impacted leaders at companies including Google, Etsy, ABC, Fox, and Chief. Passionate about integrative leadership, Kacey created a framework called the 7 Wheels of Leadership and the concept of Energetic Intelligence for coaches and leaders. Her workshops and keynotes have been presented at Vanderbilt University, CreativeMornings, Conference for a Cause, and the Country Music Association, among others.

A former opera singer who also studied energy healing for more than 20 years, Kacey fused chakra balancing, burlesque, and coaching into a wellness class called Chakralesque. She specializes in coaching leaders who struggle with imposter syndrome and the "not enoughs," cutting straight to the heart of who they truly are and helping them create an authentic, fully expressed life and career. She resides in New York City and Nashville, and maintains a global private practice.

"I realized that power isn't the key to love, but that self-love is the key to true power."

Kacey Cardin, PCC

kaceycardincoaching.com

chakralesque.com

advancedcoachaccelerator.com

Success

strategy

passion

design

Chapter 13

Unstoppable by Design

Candi Sterling

The most significant transformation that I have experienced in my life is evolving from the operational state of survival to navigation. This is my journey from floating through life to navigating an intentional path. Essentially, I went from being trapped by limiting beliefs to fully leveraging a grand future vision - one that is unburdened by limitations.

The Backstory

I was born in Montego Bay, Jamaica, and raised in the northeast region of the United States. Growing up, I was deeply impacted by my family's commitment to the American Dream which inspired me to become an entrepreneur.

Growing up in an immigrant family, I quickly learned that life as a non-citizen meant that many of the common privileges and rights of my peers did not apply to me. No international travel for years. Limited job scenario. Challenging college application process. No voting.

I eventually ceased to envision a life where I could truly have what I wanted. I simply had grown accustomed to many desires and dreams being out of reach. The consequence of this reality allowed for limiting beliefs to not only take root, but also thrive. However, those beliefs were not the only thing that my circumstances fueled...

They powered my *drive*.

The Not-So-Boring 20's

When I first began my professional career, I was driven by the long-instilled belief that I could be *more*.

Despite my on-paper limitations, I knew I was willing to work for the success that I wanted. However, over time, I would discover the difference between working for what serves others and working for what serves the future that I dreamed of creating for myself.

I was taking a lot of action, but not the right ones, and certainly none of my actions had a deeper purpose to back them. Perhaps, this fuzzy lack of clarity was a blessing in disguise.

Within a decade, I experienced life from many perspectives. I went from a burned-out marketing consultant, to a beauty professional exploring a creative industry, to a digital creator who had finally found her calling. Along the way, I cultivated a community, clients, and an abundance of experience.

The problem was, I hitched a ride on the shiny dreams of others, and the loss of mine was the source of my greatest suffering. Life was not about living... it was about survival.

When I first set out on my journey to build the dream career and life I had imagined, there were a few things I wish I had: a rock solid mentor, a clear path, and the resources I needed to properly communicate who I was and what I had to offer. A fuzzy mindset led to a cloudy habit of juggling clients in multiple industries. Finally, (eventually) I got it together by cultivating a vision that would be a magnetic "North Star," the center of keeping me focused and on track.

The greatest keys to my healing were deeply rooted in personal growth, reflection, and constantly pushing myself beyond my comfort level to enter new zones of awareness.

Through deep personal exploration I discovered that I no longer want to go with the flow. Now, I want to navigate with purpose. I got clear on my passion and potential.

The Power of Presence

In my self-awareness journey, I learned how to truly be present. The day I discovered this, it was raining hard.

Since I was so present, my new understanding was a visceral evaluation of my life. I knew right away which scenes I wanted to schedule asap, which scenes felt pleasant, which I wanted to reshoot, and which I wanted to delete entirely. I felt everything. I had to listen and practice the art of being present. Although there was a degree of discomfort, I was not experiencing suffering because it was my choice to be there.

I realized that the suffering I had experienced in the past was caused by allowing myself to be dragged in any direction others see fit for themselves. My suffering had been cultivated by others using me as a "tool," a means to their own ends not my own intention. I allowed this because I was handicapped by a "default living" mindset which flourished in my role as an immigrant with limited options. The default mindset unknowingly enslaved my mind and manifested powerfully in the layout of my life. I wanted the mindset to end as badly as the rain.

Intention: Your Vision is Your North Star

I believe that self-awareness unlocks the potential to be more tomorrow than you are today. I always knew that I needed a website, business cards, great photos online... but it was not until years later that I truly realized the full breadth of a personal brand.

I cannot stress enough how important it is to take the time to follow your passions (and sometimes even your fears) to discover what you really are meant to do.

Just because you can do many things adequately does not make them your purpose. It makes you a multi-talented person with a diverse skill set.

Your Success Story Begins Within

I believe stories do more than simply inspire us in the moment. Stories penetrate our consciousness in ways that influence our actions on the deepest level.

I wanted to create a platform that would help women on a mission to thrive. In my own life, personal branding has helped me achieve goals that I set for myself and my business endeavors.

Creating Your New Narrative

In my own transformation, I became happier and my work was more meaningful. Finally, I was beginning to release limiting beliefs. Beliefs around money, asking for help, being a perfectionist, and setting boundaries.

Part of messaging that can be difficult is communicating a message when you don't know what to say. Take an action (no matter how small) that puts you closer to your goal.

To me, personal branding was always so important because I believe that you get what you put out there. It was never an arbitrary focus for me. It played a huge role in the opportunities I attracted. As part of this branding process, vision became central.

Visualization helps you create true clarity and avoid spending time and money on things that are not truly aligned with what you want and where you want to go.

About Candi

Candi Sterling is a personal brand strategist and the founder of OnHerMission.com. Her business helps female experts create higher demand for their offerings and expertise. A public speaker and women's empowerment advocate, she recently held the title of International Ms. Jamaica 2019, earning a top 3 spot (first runner-up) in the final competition.

Candi was born in Montego Bay, Jamaica, and is currently based in Fairfield County, Connecticut. With more than 12 years of experience in branding and marketing, her communications knowledge spans several sectors including commercial real estate, the creative industries, environmental sustainability, the health foods industry, and conference/event production. Her formal education includes a master of science in library, information science, and technology from Simmons University. She is also a former Singularity University Teaching Fellow (NASA Ames Research Park).

"Stories do more than simply inspire us in the moment. Stories penetrate our consciousness in ways that influence our actions on the deepest level."

Candi Sterling

candisterling.com

Chapter 14

Your Transformation POTION

Maryann Cruz

Success and transformation! Is there an app for that? It's 2020 and there are more than 8 million apps used globally. Gadgets and quick fixes exist for just about everything. So, why isn't there an app for success and transformation? There's no app, but I have a potion.

Have you ever caught yourself wondering, am I enough? Am I...

- Smart enough?

- Tough enough?

- Courageous enough?

- Experienced enough?

I did. In fact, I struggled with that for too long. As I reflect on my journey and share how I evolved beyond self-doubt, here's another question: Have you ever met someone who makes life seem so grand and simple that it causes you to take inventory of your own life? I have.

Witnessing others reaching career and business success was so inspiring, it gave me hope that I, too, could conquer my fears and be successful. You think, *"Heck, if she can do it, so can I! I simply need to commit to it and do it."*

But my life was too different from theirs. Imagine, you're working for a Fortune 500 company, one in which many wish they worked. As an employee, you enjoy your work, the people, the stability, and, therefore, you give it 110%. However, one day you realize the more you do, the more people expect of you. Soon the 40-hour work week turns into a 60-hour work week, and you see your family in passing. You get home, cook, eat dinner, get the kids ready for bed, and ensure that everyone is prepared for the next day - all so you can start the process all over again.

You miss important events, such as your child's birthday and family milestones. That was me!

My yearning for success had me in a rut and was severely impacting my family. It got to the point that instead of looking forward to work, I was looking forward to the weekends. I was exhausted, but I still kept pushing. Surely, I was enough, since I was the one whose reliability and strategic focus the team depended on. I could've continued my path, denying my own calling. Or could I?

Things began rapidly changing at work. I had four new bosses in a two-year period. Each time, I found I had to prove myself, yet again! Then there was mention of international travel for the team; this would have me traveling abroad. How could I ask this of my family? My work already spilled over into my weekends and my family dynamic had changed. Now, with the understanding that I would be traveling more, they would feel abandoned. The questions my kids asked me were echoes of my own questions as a child: "Mom, where are you going now? Why are you always working? But Mom, it's Saturday, why are you working again?"

Concerned with how my traveling would affect my family, I sat with my husband for a heart-to-heart talk. To call that talk a "vigorous discussion" would be putting it lightly. This was the kind of spill-your-guts moment that destroys some marriages. When he heard more travel in the coming months, it threw him for a loop. That was natural, considering he had just stopped his daily commute from Connecticut to New York City, and was working remotely (while absorbing the financial impact of that decision) in an effort to bring some balance to our lives.

While we were both airing our feelings, something he said brought me white-light clarity: "Maryann, what's the return on your investment at work? You have more than 20 years of business experience in helping others in their businesses, and I hear you giving away all your knowledge for FREE! What about the passion you've always had to be an entrepreneur? You always start and stop, start and...why the heck are you still working for someone else?"

Wow! There it was! At this rate, would I break down or have a breakthrough?

We can't justify all our sacrifices, forever. It's when you realize the promise you made to yourself of always being there for your children is quickly dissipating that you make a different choice. That day had arrived for me. That was the day I said: *Enough is enough!*

It instantly became a silent revelation. I didn't need to give explanations. I said goodbye to my colleagues and finally followed the path that was meant to be.

I was able to see clearly. I'd been overcompensating. As a child, I had often been negatively compared to others regarding my physical appearance, my personality, and everything under the sun. Figuring then that I wouldn't survive on my looks, I turned to books and worked my hardest at doing everything to perfection. I thought being the same straight-A student in adulthood would bring me success. But it hadn't. That perfectionism led me to analysis paralysis, fear of failure, fear of success (yes, this is real), self-sabotage, and my struggle with impostor syndrome. The fear that I wasn't enough.

Having awakened, the true work began. I had to decide what success meant to ME. It was one of those moments when you realize that, in your life journey, you have gained valuable insight and you not only have enough to be successful, you also have enough to share with the world. I was ready to win! Which meant... what?

Well, success and transformation can only be defined by YOU! Your core beliefs and values will determine how you define success and transformation. Success to me meant family, building my business, and empowering myself and others. I took inventory: I had the skills (hard and soft), knowledge, tech expertise, corporate experience, strategy, budgeting - you name it! I was willing to invest. I had a consuming passion and hunger to succeed! I immediately started networking and leading women's groups and workshops. You have to dive in! I succeeded in making the leap. You can do it, too. But first, consider this.

Do you quantify success by:

- the amount of time you have by yourself or with your family?

- your annual income?

- your travel and adventures?

What about transformation, is it:

- how you look or feel?

- how connected you are with spirit?

- or a change in mindset?

While there isn't an app for transformation, I do have a POTION to share.

P - Follow your *passion*; find your *purpose*; embrace your *power*. As a child, you were curious and occasionally the explorer. It's instinctual. Most parents know this. There were certain things you loved doing, perhaps arts, crafts, sports, writing, telling stories, giving friends advice, etc... As you got older, there were expectations of how you should behave, engage, and lead your life. As an adult, there are even more expectations of how you should live and again, lead your life.

The keyword here is "your." It is YOUR life. Therefore, why would you allow others to influence how YOU live it? Take some time to reflect on your past. What were you passionate or excited about then? What brings this same level of energy to you now? What makes you unique? What is your gift or superpower? Then ask yourself, "What's holding me back?" Overcome that obstacle. When you find your passion and live it, you realize it's your true purpose, and in that purpose, you embrace your power.

O - Be *open-minded* and *optimistic*, and *opportunities* will *overflow*. Have you ever had a friend who was an "Eeyore"? Just like the Winnie-the-Pooh character, this person is a pessimist, gloomy, and depressed? When you see their name pop up on your phone, you debate whether or not to answer the call, as you automatically feel your energy depleting? Why is this? Well, it's simple; pessimists have a scarcity mindset which often means the person is insecure and fearful of taking risks and following their dreams.

With the world as challenging as it is, most people turn to optimists for guidance. Optimists have an abundant mindset and according to Stephen Covey's, *The Seven Habits of Highly Effective People*, "abundance mentality" flows out of a deep inner sense of personal worth and security. There is plenty out there and enough to spare for everyone.

As a result, being open-minded and optimistic leads to a larger network of like-minded people who enable you to succeed.

T - For ***transformation to transcend***, you must face your ***truths***. There are wounds which seem timeless; however, you must set aside the time to do the inner work. Doing the inner work will allow you to understand who you are, what your ***triggers*** are, how to tune into your emotions and change your thinking, so you may thrive. While most people define triggers on a personal level, given past personal experiences, triggers also impact leaders and entrepreneurs on the business level. To succeed, you must know your strengths and weaknesses. What are your triggers in business? What's holding you back? Is it one thing or a multitude of things?

Up to my breakthrough, I would find myself following my passion into exciting ventures but would stop myself prior to launch! Why? Well, I hadn't done the inner work. I couldn't pinpoint what was holding me back. I didn't know what my triggers were in order to change my mindset and actions. If you fall off of cloud nine the minute someone says a particular thing, that's a trigger. Unknowingly, that individual said something that evoked an unpleasant emotion from your past resulting in you feeling threatened, insecure, or anxious. Be self-aware and you'll know what those are.

I - There will be moments when you have difficult decisions to make. In those instances, it's essential to embrace your *intuition*. You have the answers within YOU. Yes, YOU! But there will be moments in which you'd like validation. In those instances, know it's OK to share your thoughts with your tribe. Additionally, know that it's OK to invest in yourself. **Invest** in the tools, resources, and experts you need to gain and keep momentum.

O - Embrace your *originality*! No one else has walked in your shoes; therefore, they cannot fully share your journey, provide you perspective on things, or share your gifts. This is something exclusively for YOU to do. While the world is filled with competitors, the world is also filled with opportunities. Why? Well, because while what you may offer is similar to that of your competitors, there's a great difference in the way you uniquely engage with everyone. It's the synergy!

N – **Nurture** your relationships with family, friends, clients, partnerships and, most importantly, yourself. In the pursuit of success and in the midst of transformation, there is a great deal that happens and many decisions to make. There will be instances where you will need to prioritize among several commitments in a day, sometimes in an hour. It's moments like these where nurturing your relationships are essential. When people know who you are, what your mission, vision, and goals are, as well as your character, they will respect your decisions. It's OK to say *no*.

It's also OK to say yes! Yes to yourself, the things you enjoy doing, and the activities that will help you refill your cup.

As you can imagine, overcoming my challenges didn't happen overnight, but it did happen over time by my being tuned in to my emotions and thoughts, and especially by dispelling my fears. Take a minute to consider how you handle fear? Do you walk in faith? I certainly do.

I also **F**irst **E**ducate myself on the situation **A**nd then **R**espond. Handle fear and avoid mistakes with a thought-out response. When someone says something that makes you feel uncertain, frustrated, or scared, take a minute to think of the root cause of this feeling. Then, face it, and let it go. Being able to face your truth and let everything else go allows you to grow.

There will be moments in life that will have you questioning whether or not you're making the right decision. In those moments remember life is full of options and you're the boss of the way you choose to live your life.

As a business strategist and coach, I ask the difficult questions that are essential in bringing clarity to my clients. Once you are clear on what your vision is for your life and business, it's much easier to develop a strategic roadmap to success. While I share the POTION with you, it's also important to know that the ingredients for success will be a little different for you than they are for me. They vary from person to person. Remember, success is not only defined by you but also by your past, your passion, your purpose, and your power. Reflect, redefine, and embrace your transformational journey!

About Maryann

Maryann Cruz is a business strategist and coach and co-founder of C3 Collaborative, LLC. Maryann assists creatives and passionate entrepreneurs to gain clarity and momentum in business through the development of thorough strategies, action plans, and accountability. Maryann is an entrepreneur's co-pilot to success.

After spending 20+ years in all facets of business operations, Maryann knows what is truly required to succeed in business beyond entrepreneurial passion. Recognizing the importance of building a solid business foundation to achieve one's vision and guiding creatives through this essential process is where she thrives.

"Having awakened, the true work began.
I had to decide what success meant to ME."

Maryann Cruz

www.maryanncruz.co

Chapter 15

Aligned by Design

Kristi H. Sullivan

What if I told you that to achieve success, you didn't have to work as hard, or be as tired, struggling or overwhelmed, as you might be feeling right now - and that authentically living your best life could be a lot easier and feel effortless? Would you believe that it's possible - or would you call me crazy, a dreamer, or unrealistic? OR could you consider the potential that working less for more success is possible?

Let me share with you how it's possible, how I personally experienced it, and how it transformed me.

I am a first-generation American citizen whose parents were Eastern European - the typical hard-working natives who believed not only in shedding blood, sweat, and tears, but also in the idea that life was meant to be hard, and that nothing came easy, especially success without hard work. To be honest, it's a doctrine that has been passed down through many generations in my family - and perhaps yours, too.

I remember being the age of five and waiting impatiently down our street at the yellow fire hydrant for my dad to drive up on his way home from work, where he would pull over in his Toyota, and open the door for me to hop in the passenger seat. Then I'd slide over to sit on his lap so I could "drive" the car home, which entailed me holding on to the steering wheel while he controlled the gas and brake pedals. The actual distance was just a few houses, but it was the best few minutes (OK, probably seconds) of my day.

It not only felt exhilarating to drive the car at the mere age of 5, but I was excited to spend a few one-on-one minutes with my father who had worked a full day at his engineering job only to arrive home for a quick dinner with the family before exiting to the garage or yard to start his second job of working on house projects most every night. You could say my father literally built our house with his bare hands - and a lot of blood, sweat, and tears (the latter mainly from my mother who missed his time and attention with her).

It's no surprise that I was "conditioned" to believe that success only came with hard work, and that my path to the future followed a typical formula: study hard, graduate, and go to college, study hard more, graduate, and get a job, work hard until you retire... then reap the reward - when you're tired and worn out! This was the formula that I was predestined to follow thanks to my ancestral fate.

However, somewhere along the way, I started to hear other voices and messages that questioned these concepts, and that eventually led to transformation in my life.

One day in particular, about three years ago, I received an email from my friend, Linda, that included a video entitled "Three Lies and One Life-Changing Truth That No One is Talking About." It caught my attention and, almost immediately, I watched the video and contacted her to learn more about a new unconventional coaching program that she was launching with her partner, Michael. It came at the right time because I had been questioning how hard I felt like I had to work to get ahead, such as taking on more responsibility at a nonprofit job to try to get paid more, and how much effort was needed to make things happen, like the extra hours I put into growing a side business that I recently started. And most of the time, without the pay or pay-off I desired. Wasn't there an easier way to achieve success and manifest abundance - like taking a blue pill for the blissful ignorance that I yearned for instead of the red pill for the unpleasant truth of my kin?

Let me explain the pill reference... in the sci-fi movie *The Matrix*, the character Morpheus offers a choice to the hero, Neo, who is questioning the reality (or rather illusion) of life: "This is your last chance. After this, there is no turning back. You take the blue pill - the story ends, you wake up in your bed and believe whatever you want to believe. You take the red pill - you stay in Wonderland, and I show you how deep the rabbit hole goes. Remember: all I'm offering is the truth. Nothing more."

Spoiler alert: Neo takes the red pill and wakes up from the world of conditioned illusion to the real-world Matrix.

After I spoke to Linda, I embarked on a journey with her and Michael over the next two years that took our coaching group down what we called the rabbit hole. The program introduced us to the Human Design system, the foundation of our coaching. It was a life-changing concept for me which revealed the indoctrination that I had learned in life and the conditioning that had been passed down from generation to generation through my hard-working Polish and Lithuanian roots. This new Matrix-type training also opened up my awareness to the social conditioning that I, like most of us, receive from mass influencers, such as teachers, authority figures, advertising spokespersons, and even celebrities. This conditioned "brainwashing" often encourages a one-size-fits-all in areas like education, work, habits, attitudes, and life in general, and may even pressure us to compare ourselves to others. However, the Human Design theory helped me understand my unique energetic blueprint, how I was encoded at birth, and what was my natural state versus a learned one - although I am still vulnerable to the conscious and unconscious influence of outside forces or voices.

And how does this relate to transformation, manifesting abundance, and achieving success? I began to realize that putting in extra effort at work didn't necessarily equal more income, and that extra hours in my side hustle didn't immediately have the results for which I was hoping. My conditioned way of thinking would declare, *"But you haven't put in enough time or effort, you must do more - maybe you're just not doing it right and need to try harder, perhaps be more patient, or fail more to learn the lessons to get further."*

Now hold on, and just stop that old stinkin' thinkin'! If working hard paid off for everyone the same, then wouldn't more of us be living an abundant life??

Another important concept I learned during my coaching program was that the mind is not the best place for solving problems or making decisions. In fact, thinking can often produce confusion, indecision, and resistance. According to Human Design, the head and third eye (or ajna) energy centers take in inspiration, visualizations, and concepts - we receive information here only for research and processing. Rather, our wisdom for decision making resides with the intuition, gut feelings, or emotional energy situated in the body, below the head. This means that getting out of the head and into the body is critical for tapping into our deeper wisdom, beyond the intellect. Human Design is a "how to manual" for accessing the wisdom that exists outside of the mind and deep within oneself. To access this, daily self-care activity is essential for tapping into your wisdom centers in the body. And to stop the stinkin' thinkin'!

Daily self-care is essential not only for well-being but for helping to align your energy. I found that the more I made self-care a priority, the more I accessed my inner wisdom and the more I received opportunities that led to success. It seemed the less hard I worked, the more effortless things became - as long as I recognized my energetic design and made the effort to stay aligned. The work was on the inside, not the outside!

Thanks to my training, I now understand that my ability to manifest abundance is a direct result of aligning my effort and my energy with my true, natural design with which I was encoded. By living in alignment with my unique Human Design, I create more opportunities and invitations for success and abundance. Unlearning my conditioning and living in an unconditioned way is a new formula, and to do so is a daily practice and takes consistent self-care. With this new formula, I was able to transition from the hard work of my former career and step more fully into my passion of working in wellness and supporting women in their self-care journey, along with teaching Human Design. And this new career feels effortless and in alignment with my true design - a life-changing transformation!

I now blend my background in communications and marketing with my interest and expertise in health and well-being. My mission is to guide and motivate busy women to give themselves permission to make essential self-care a priority and to curate daily rituals that fit their lifestyle (and Human Design) through a virtual membership platform and network of resources and tools. And I am excited to share the Human Design system through workshops and individual sessions with clients who want to understand their unique energetic blueprint.

Now, here's the question I suggest for you to answer - with your body, and not your mind - are you going to take the blue pill or the red pill?

By the way, when I Googled *The Matrix* and the blue versus red pill story, I came across a similar reference in the 2013 movie, *The Secret Life of Walter Mitty*. When Walter, played by Ben Stiller, is at the airport in Greenland, he asks the booth attendant: "Do you have any cars available?" The man replies, "Yeah, we have a blue one and a red one." Walter responds, "I'll take the red one."

In my research, I also found a reference to a May 2020 tweet by Elon Musk stating, "Take the red pill," a response to a Twitter user which meant taking a "free-thinking attitude and waking up from a normal life of sloth and ignorance."

I recommend you choose the red pill, too - and experience effortless success, manifested abundance, and transformation!

About Kristi

Kristi H. Sullivan is a wellness advocate and self-care expert with a passion for health, wealth, and happiness and for helping women thrive in these areas. She hosts a virtual community to help busy women give themselves permission to make self-care a priority and to help them curate daily rituals that fit their lifestyle. In addition, she teaches workshops and does readings on Human Design and the art of aligning with your true self to authentically live your best life and manifest abundance.

Kristi is also a co-author of the *Ultimate Guide to Self-Healing, Volume 2,* and *The Great Pause: Blessings & Wisdom from COVID-19* (both written and published during the 2020 pandemic).

"Unlearning our conditioning and living in an unconditioned way is a new formula, and to do so is a daily practice and takes consistent self-care."

Kristi H. Sullivan

kristiselfcare.com

Inspire(d)

recovery

awakening

rise

divine

invitation

Chapter 16

From Suffering to Grace

Robin H. Clare

Living As An Addict

For 40 years, I struggled with obsessive-compulsive food disorder and bulimia. While that might have seemed like an incredibly long time, it felt like an instant when it became part of my everyday living. My day would begin most often with a healthy breakfast, but as soon as I ate something that I perceived to be "bad," the mania would begin.

The conversation with my inner addict would be endless all day long. *"What are you eating?" "Is it healthy?" "How much can you eat before you have to purge?" "Stop eating – you are such a disappointment." "You purged again – this is so humiliating."* I became the victim of my life through obsessive eating and the persecutor of my life through bulimia. I was slowly committing suicide.

Long-Term Health Issues

I knew in my mind and my heart that what I was doing could have long-term implications on my health, but I could not stop. It was my way of life, and I became good at hiding my daily rituals of overeating and purging. An important point about food addicts is that we are allowed (by society) to eat three meals a day plus snacks. So, why even bother to call food disorders and bulimia an addiction?

Yet, the obesity levels in our country are out of control. According to the CDC, over 40% of the population of the United States is obese. Obesity leads to diabetes, heart disease, and many other ailments. I would not recommend purging as a way to lose weight. People who purge are not thin - just the opposite. By purging, our body moves into starvation mode, not knowing where nutrition is coming from next. Therefore, all calories are held as storage of fat in the body.

I had dear friends who I would envy as they were able to stay in long-term recovery from any substance or vice addiction. I would classify the ones in recovery for over 20 years as in remission from addiction. As I looked at others in recovery, I would wonder, *"why not me?"* There had to be an essential knowledge about addiction that I was missing.

What Was I Addicted To?

It might have appeared that I was addicted to overeating and bulimia. In actuality, I was addicted to suffering. The obsessive eating and the bulimia were secondary addictions that I had manifested as a result of my painful experiences. I had experienced childhood, teen, and adult trauma that had created emotional patterns that remained unhealed. Suffering is defined as wallowing in your pain. For 40 years, I did not know I was suffering and, therefore, I did not realize I was wallowing, and I did not know that I needed to heal my suffering to come into recovery.

The Successful Addict

Like many of the 30 million people in the United States with eating disorders, I became a successful person. I made it through college, graduate school, 25 years in corporate America, 10 years as a spiritual entrepreneur, and as a highly-valued wife and mother. Most people who read my current book were shocked. How could Robin Clare be an addict? I have often asked myself that question and have concluded that this was all part of an incredible spiritual journey that has resulted in my recovery and a mission to serve humanity. This mission was presented to me by the Holy Spirit, or Sophia as she identified herself.

Sophia's Request

Sophia came face-to-face with me at the end of a healing session while I was in a meditative state. In my meditation, I had just emerged from a cleansing waterfall, and I stood in the still water at its base. A beautiful Being of Light came walking towards me. She said, "I am Sophia." I wanted to bow my head in reverence, but I could not take my eyes off her face.

When she first stepped in front of me, her face was one of a young maiden, then she aged before my eyes through every stage of a woman's life, including becoming an elder. It seemed that she was every woman merged into one Being of Light. I quickly said to myself, "*Stop staring and listen; she must have something important to tell you.*"

Sophia continued, "I have been speaking to you since you were 17-years-old, preparing you to write a book, and I will be your guide. The name of this book is *Feast & Famine, Healing Addiction with Grace*. The book will be your story of addiction and how you have healed your addiction through a deep dedication to your spiritual path."

Just One Major Problem

While I was deeply honored to receive this request from Sophia, I was still in addiction. I decided I would fake it until I made it. That never happened. I wrote my first draft of *Feast &*

Famine in addiction, and at the end of the book I wanted to write, *"Well, I hope these teachings work for you because they didn't work for me."* I put the book down and knew I was not ready to publish it. Nor was I prepared to come into recovery; that would take a message from my deceased grandmother.

In a conversation with a spiritually gifted client, my grandmother arrived to talk with me. She said that if I did not bury my bulimia, my family would bury me. I believed her, yet, I chose to have one more pig out and one more episode of bulimia. I compared myself to an alcoholic needing one more glass of wine before stopping drinking.

This difference between the alcoholic and me was that my last episode almost killed me. After violent retching, my nose began to bleed significantly, and I had severe pain all over my body. I had never experienced either of these two symptoms, and I knew that I was getting ready to have a fatal bulimic incident if I did not stop that day. I was finally done after 40 years. Still, a significant part of my healing was unfolding.

The Examined Life

Of course, stopping the addicted behavior was paramount, but to sustain long-term recovery, one must heal the source of their initial suffering. For me, this required a combination of mental health therapy, energy healing, and a combination of Western and Eastern medicines. I also needed to stay deeply connected to my inner wisdom and my spiritual team. I achieved this through meditation, prayer, and an occasional reading from a gifted messenger.

As a result of examining my life, I discovered that I had two emotional patterns that were blocking my success. The first pattern was a fear of being humiliated in public. In this lifetime, I had been humiliated in public over 20 times, beginning at 6-years-old. The second pattern was a fear of persecution that I had brought forth from past lives. The solution for me became not allowing anyone to have the role of a judge in my life. If I do not give them that power, they could not humiliate or persecute me.

The Play Is Closed

My teachers from the Oneness University, Sri Amma and Sri Bhagavan, said that the most important relationship to heal in our lives is the one with our parents. We chose our parents before our incarnation to give us an equal dose of love and pain, but the scale can easily sway to one side or the other.

To stay grounded in recovery, I had to heal my relationship with my parents. My dad was easy; I could chat with him in the spiritual realm. My mom was harder; she embraced her role as body judge for me. I had to tell her that the play on Robin's body was now closed, and we needed to find other topics to talk about. My body and my weight were off-limits as conversation topics.

Sophia's Divine Healing Path

With my recovery grounded in my day-to-day life, I could rewrite and release *Feast & Famine* and present the profound divine healing path that Sophia desired to share with humanity. Her healing path consisted of four spiritual concepts that one must live to stay grounded in recovery. Here is a brief summary of each of the four steps.

Pain Is Inevitable. If we agree that we are composed of mind, body, spirit, and emotion, then we have four major areas where we can incur pain. Because we are an integrated system, pain in one area creates unease in the other three. Pain of some sort is inevitable in our day-to-day experience as a human being.

Suffering Is An Option. Somewhere in our popular culture, we have put these two words together: "pain and suffering." If suffering is an option, then why is it connected to pain, which is inevitable? Can you think of someone who is in pain, but is not suffering? More likely, you can think of many people who are in pain and who are suffering.

Surrender Is Required. It is hard to think of someone who is in pain who is not suffering. We are surrounded by many people who are in pain and who are suffering, perhaps, even ourselves. The good news is the path to get out of the pain and suffering is surrender. Surrender means to throw up your hands and implore with all the conviction you can gather, "Divine, I am done with this pain and suffering – please help me!"

Grace Must Be Allowed. While you may focus on the word "Grace" in this phrase, the word "allowed" is the essential part of the phrase. The question you must ask yourself is, are you truly done with the pain and suffering that you have been experiencing? Because if not, you are not in surrender, and, therefore, Grace will not be allowed in. If you are indeed done with pain and suffering, and you are genuinely in surrender, then Grace will come to ease your pain.

Serving Others

With *Feast & Famine* in hand, I began speaking on podcasts and radio shows and at group events. I could have quickly dedicated my life to sharing Sophia's Divine Healing Path. However, I was motivated to expand my work to include a direction that began with an interesting question from my spirit guides. They asked, "Do you think spiritual people have lived such extraordinary lives for their own entertainment?"

Of course not! Spiritual people are here to teach others about how they have transformed on their life journey. As an author of three spiritual self-help books, I knew that I would serve others well as a writing coach, helping others to share their incredible story of transformation.

From the moment we incarnated into this physical vessel, our Soul has been leading the way, enabling our life to unfold in perfect order. You have a life story that has filled your days with thought-provoking events and outcomes. These events are not always glamorous; in fact, they might be filled with drama and trauma.

Our life experiences consist of good, bad, and ugly moments. All three of these types of experiences make for excellent teaching material in your personal life and professional life. These same experiences make for incredible content when writing your life story.

Everyone should write their life story, whether they ever want to publish it or not. By writing your life story, you will gain a greater understanding of what has transpired in your life. This review will enable you to see where you have healed and take stock of all that you have accomplished. This review will also point out where you still need to improve your life.

There are many different ways to heal your life, and one of the most profound ways is to engage in a conversation with your inner wisdom. By writing your story, you activate your inner wisdom, and you see your traumatic patterns and where profound healing is possible. Writing and sharing your life story takes a tremendous amount of courage. I salute my fellow contributors of this book for their bravery. What I know for sure is that when you write your life story, you heal yourself. When you share your life story with others, you heal them.

About Robin

Only after revealing her deepest dark secret, Robin H. Clare was able to become her most authentic, spiritual self. Struggling with food addiction and bulimia for decades, she finally dug deep into current and past lives to heal wounds that had blocked success and fed her active addiction. Now in recovery, Robin is living her Soul Mission as a speaker and life and writing coach.

As an author, she documented her extraordinary spiritual journey in the highly-acclaimed *Messiah Within*, followed by Amazon bestsellers, *The Divine Keys*, and *Feast & Famine*. Awards include 10 Best Life/Business Coaches and 10 Best Energy Healers in The Natural Nutmeg Readers Polls of 2017-2019.

"From the moment we incarnated into this physical vessel, our Soul has been leading the way, enabling our life to unfold in perfect order."

Robin H. Clare

www.clare-ity.com

Chapter 17

Finding Primal Love

Mary Roy

I do not remember opening my eyes that morning, but I must have because the rest of the day ensued. Momentum within each day was my intent and the lifeline that held my head above water. Two weeks earlier, I had received life-altering news. All that I knew had been turned upside down and any stability I was able to muster in my legs or any part of my body felt heroic. *Just get up and get moving* became my unspoken motto. The lack of clarity associated with my future brought concern and panic.

Outside the sun rose, shining light onto boats nestled in the harbor and then into my window, waking me. I enjoyed its warmth, if only for a moment, then reality hit. Digging deep, I found courage and met the beckoning day. Sticking to the plan, I lifted my unwilling body from the bed adorned with blue and white sailboat sheets, slipped on black running tights, and zipped my sports jacket in preparation for a walk.

While leaving the enclosure of my tiny seashell-filled, fully furnished, and perfectly decorated rental nestled on the Connecticut River, the dazed veil of uneasiness overshadowing my everyday life, lifted, just a bit.

Snow had fallen through the night. Not your average snow; this was eight inches of glistening white powder succumbing to the brilliance of the morning sun. It beamed a warming presence upon its whiteness, turning fluffy to slushy, without a hint of dirt as you might expect. Simply a shiny bright lustrous pulp, my Nikes happily shared the cement.

Not only were my running shoes pleased to encounter this magical morning, my whole body, every cell, was delighted. The crisp clean air filled my lungs. The microscopic droplets of water lingering in the air adding moisture to my skin while the sun's rays warmed my whole being from the outside in, then the inside out.

The beauty of this moment, served to me on what appeared to be a silver platter, pronounced by the artistry of Mother Nature, charmed my being and stunned the trapping of distress ruling my life into a present moment of lucidity. My labored breath left; silence entered. I could hear everything everywhere for miles and miles, lifetimes upon lifetimes and all that is buried in the dirt of all the world and carried in the leaves of all the trees came to me in one tiny second, a blink, a minute glimpse of time that carried all that is. Stillness beyond stillness.

This moment wrapped in beauty bigger than all of life caught me by surprise, astounded my core, and brought me deeper into the here and now than I had ever been. With this I forgot all else; I knew there was nothing else.

The darkened constraint of my life was forgotten.

The news, stage three breast cancer; forgotten. Three weeks after divorce; forgotten. My sister Ann, dad, uncle, and grandfather's death from cancer, forgotten. Packing up 21 years of living including all things personal and a business to relocate and begin again at 54; forgotten.

I forgot and slipped into the grace and eternity of the splendor around me. As I snapped out of fear, I was reminded of life and of love, eternal love.

The air entering my body felt cleaner than any I had ever breathed, and I knew I was sharing it with all creatures throughout time. Somehow, they were all there with me in that tiny historic village on the river. I suddenly felt supported, whole, and stronger than I had in quite some time.

Pratt Street, quieter than usual, offered the gift of space and time allowing a new perception to enter my consciousness. With mind, body, and soul fully prepped and opened by the surroundings Mother Nature had provided, the Universe, God, my Higher Self, whatever that entity is that speaks to you, spoke to me. The message was clear and concise. *Heal your cancer naturally. You are on a journey that began many years ago. This is what you are here for. Go to the mountains. Sit in the hills, walk the peaks, get to know the people. South America, shamans, solitude; whatever it takes. Like the monk with the long dreadlocks in the film Baraka, seek ancient teachings and text. This is who you are; this is your path. Whatever the outcome, life or death. Separate from your modern-day world and go within. Heal your life. Heal your cancer. It will come from a path not expected. Do not push. Learn to surrender. Wisdom and beauty will come. Go there in peace and know everything will be okay.*

Clear, vivid, and full of truth, all I could do was let the message enter my being. I continued my walk to the water's edge, through the narrow side streets, and to the cemetery perched on the bank of the river. Heal naturally, of course this would be my path, it made the utmost sense.

All the books I had read through the years on health, wellness, and the effects of the mind on the body had led me here. My dad's cancer ravaging his body at 48 years of age had always seemed to me more of a product of his mind and challenging life circumstances rather than the nature of any chemicals he had been exposed to or the genes he was born with. My sister Ann's story was wrought with struggle as well. I was a fitness professional drawn to all things holistic with a curiosity for the mystical. Yes, this was it, of course it was, this was my journey.

Returning to my tiny waterside abode, my direction was clear. Fueled with the passion and confidence that comes with a known pathway, I could breathe easier. My future seemed manageable. I knew how to begin. I had clarity.

Or did I?

Fascinating how I can be so sure about my path in one moment and then experience so much turmoil and indecision in the next. The answer to why this is so, I am sure, lies in this quote from Eckhart Tolle.

You find peace not by rearranging the circumstances
of your life, but by realizing who you are at the deepest level.
Eckhart Tolle

All that needs to be done is to replace the word "peace" with "healing." In fact, healing and peace are synonymous. On that morning in Essex, CT, my journey to healing began as an arrangement of circumstances. My choice of how to heal was set in motion. That was the easy part. What was yet to come, the realization of who I was at the deepest level, would prove to be the most challenging endeavor of my life.

Before being diagnosed with breast cancer, my plan was to open a fitness studio designed to redefine the philosophies associated with fitness. Being a personal trainer and group fitness instructor in Los Angeles and in New England for decades, I sensed a growing need for a different approach. The pursuit of the perfect body, thin thighs, a flat stomach, or fitting in to a societal norm was no longer motivating for many women. They were searching for deeper meaning and purpose. Many were looking simply to feel good in their body, release tension, find peace, and live in their truth. I could relate to this desire and was interested in being part of this new paradigm ready to emerge in the world of fitness.

Personally, working with a life coach, we named my future fitness company Primal Love Studio. The name stirred something deep inside me. My goal was to be brave enough to own a studio with that name, move to the Lower East Side of Manhattan, and dive deep into teaching self-expression, authenticity, and optimal well-being through movement. I looked forward to meeting other women willing to break through the boundaries of normalcy that would join me on this path. My life coach's goal for me varied from mine. She challenged me to discover the meaning of Primal Love. My vision appeared much more fun than hers. Nonetheless, I agreed.

My journey began with a Google search of the meaning and origins of these words; little did I know that the Universe had something much more involved planned for me than a number one ranking of the word "primal."

My feisty life coach kept pushing, though she would refer to it as guiding, and I was ready and more than willing. Prior to my divorce, I was aware that my life had gotten far off track. I had lost myself in the world of parenting three beautiful girls, while trying to hold together a structure of *the perfect life*. I no longer knew who I was, and I became unclear on where to even find me. I now know this to be the perfect breeding ground for disease. And as it went, in walked cancer.

My life-threatening diagnosis, desire to heal naturally, and search for the meaning of *primal love* became the *perfect storm* to dive deep into a world so far from the control and lack of surrender I had grown accustomed to living. To heal naturally, I would need to address not only the physical aspect of my disease, but what I have come to know as more imperative and inescapable, the role that mental, emotional, and spiritual well-being play in illness. What first appeared as merely a scary diagnosis, an obstacle to overcome, became the catalyst to heal at a profound level and grow my life to a deeper more meaningful place.

In lieu of four months of chemotherapy, six weeks of radiation, 10 months of a Her2 specific drug pumped into my body via a port, and 10 years of an estrogen blocker, I dove in and learned that codependency, the victim mentality, shadows, and the dance of narcissism, all had a strong hold on my life. This was impairing not only my happiness, but my health as well. With the desire to heal, I faced all aspects of myself with courage and self-responsibility. Uncovering the depths of my childhood pain, patterns, and shadows led me to a profound spiritual awakening that healed not only my life, but my body as well.

The realization of who I was at the deepest level, as suggested by Eckhart Tolle, came with an awakening that allowed light in to heal my physical body, and love to enter, flooding my soul and healing my spirit. I released ego and limiting beliefs to start walking in my truth. Self-love, self-acceptance, and a body that functions with optimal health and well-being were born.

This acceptance and love are the first love. The love of self. The love that all other love is born from. This is, in fact, Primal Love.

My journey went deeper than ever anticipated. For that, I am grateful. Primal Love Studio in the beginning merely sounded alluring, mystical, and empowering. That seemed to be enough for me. Now I know that it embodies all those stirring traits and much more. I am honored and privileged to bring this teaching of Primal Love through workouts, coaching, and training to anyone who seeks this path of self-empowerment and spiritual awakening. My mission is to guide others to infuse their life with an abundance of vitality, health, and passion that is born from self-love and self-acceptance.

I encourage you to join me on this fulfilling journey.

About Mary

Mary is a wellness industry veteran, certified as a group fitness instructor in Boston, Massachusetts, in the 80s, and as a personal trainer in Santa Monica, California, in the 90s. As a seasoned entrepreneur, she taught group fitness, owned a personal training company, and implemented on-line wellness programming. Fitness and swimsuit competitions were part of her early career where she was featured on ESPN and *Entertainment Tonight*.

In 2020, Mary completed a 200-hour yoga teacher certification alongside a natural healing regimen from stage three breast cancer. The intersection of these and an unwavering desire to heal her physical body, as well as her emotional and spiritual life, led her to a spiritual awakening and the creation of Primal Love Studio.

"The realization of who we are at the deepest level that comes with an awakening allows light in that heals our physical body, and love to enter that floods our soul and heals our spirit."

Mary Roy

PrimalLoveStudio.com

Chapter 18

Seven Transformation Stages to the Divine Feminine

Donna Martire Miller, MA, CIPP

"If you want to awaken all of humanity, then awaken all of yourself. If you want to eliminate the suffering in the world, then eliminate all that is dark and negative in yourself. Truly, the greatest gift you have to give is that of your own self transformation."
Lao Tzu

I was born in 1955. Everything I was experiencing at that time was geared towards the family. The world I grew up in was to a great extent a patriarchal society. I was raised to honor, look up to, and care for the men in my life, and they, in turn, would protect and support me and all the women and children in the family.

I never embraced this belief system totally. From a very young age, I knew I had a strong inquisitive desire to learn, grow, and experience the world differently than the little girls I played with. I did not fit in and for many years I felt odd and lonely. I had trouble keeping friends. There began what would lead to many years of emotional instability. I would think, *What was wrong with me?*

Rejected and bewildered, I would retreat to the familiarity of being with my siblings. My mother and father had four children together. I was the third born, having two older sisters and one baby brother. My parents also took in six foster children. When I could not find a friend, I simply went home. There were plenty of us there. We would share meals and the few television programs that we were allowed to watch, and we would play. Often there were tears turned to laughter and laughter turned to tears, but this was what I would fall back on.

I always felt this duality of energy and emotion, a strong need for connection and at the same time a strong need to fly free. Little did I know that *connection* would become a lifelong theme for me. I would live to connect many people to their purpose and to living connected to their authentic self. This would be my path. It was not on the outside of me, as I originally believed, where I would feel connection. It would be inside me all along. I know now that the intense love I hold in my heart is what makes me fly free. My heart took wings as it soared towards the life I wanted to live. A life filled with music and wonder, a life worth living!

I lived in a small town, went to a Catholic grammar school and a public high school. I had this strong wild energy that got me into a lot of trouble as a child and earned me the nickname "the daydreamer" in high school. I sat in classes compelled to dream about departing from a life that would simply lead me to be a happy homemaker. I envied women that could do that; I was not able to.

The yin and yang energies in me were equally as strong but not in harmony or balance. Again, I felt duality. My actions were yin-like, connected to the feminine desire to begin a family. I tried to abide, marrying my handsome high school sweetheart. We had two beautiful children together. My desires, however, were yang-like, and I desired to have a full-time career as a singer. I wanted to travel the world on tour as a vocalist. Well, you can imagine that this did not sit well with my husband. He gave me an ultimatum: a career as a vocalist or him. Because yin and yang are inseparable, I wanted both. The marriage did not survive this intersection of my two strong energies. I would now experience the first of several transformational challenges.

FIRST TRANSFORMATION: I must confront my own definition of what it means to be a woman.

My identity was confined by the societal norms I grew up with. I had a very strong belief system that I was challenging. I asked myself, *What does it mean to be a good woman? Was I being a good mother by uprooting my children and driving across the country with them in tow to follow this dream?* I felt shame and sadness for the loss of a true friend, my husband, and I still had the belief that for a woman to pursue a career, especially in entertainment...well, that was unfathomable for a *good* woman to do.

Shame is far reaching and caustic to self-perception. I began to hear that little voice in my head saying, *You are odd. You will never fit in. No one likes you, especially now. No one will ever love you again. You blew it.* I felt remorse. The only thing I could do now was to achieve the success I desired.

Shame, remorse, and sadness could not live in the same heart as creativity, success, and the joy of being able to share one of my God-given talents with the world. This mantra motivated me to overcome my fear of failure, my fear of being disliked or misunderstood. I would practice, I would sing, my children would see the country with me. This would be a rich experience for the kids.

My self-worth was beginning to separate from that little voice in my head. In fact, I learned to tell it to shut the hell up. That's right, this woman now felt brave and unstoppable. I was beginning to transform my belief about what it meant to be a good woman, and this fit me like my favorite pair of blue jeans.

The power of the divine feminine was continually struggling to grow and become... that fire burned in my belly constantly. I did achieve my dream. I toured this beautiful country and went overseas to Japan to sing as well.

Still, I tried again and again to focus on wearing that wedding ring and having that happy family. I married two other times. I birthed a third beautiful child. Both marriages ended badly. I had not married for any of the right reasons. I married because of my own limiting beliefs.

SECOND TRANSFORMATION: *Comparing myself to other women was not healthy. I had to stop.*

I suppose it is human to compare ourselves to other women. The music business was heavily reinforcing this very harmful belief that beauty was skin deep. I had starved myself into a double o clothing size yet still was told to lose just five more pounds before the next show. The voice in my head was having a field day. I did not fit in as a wife, and my body was just not going to fit the music business standards for success either. At a whopping 105 pounds, I was considered fat.

I reached out to my siblings and my old friends. I just wanted to go home. Back across the country we went. I was disillusioned. I had to confront a new set of difficult emotions. I was again alone and lonely. One day as I sat by the phone with no one to call, I turned to faith and, for the first time in many years, I prayed. My go-to resources at this level of transformation were reconnecting to old and trusted friends, family, and God.

My children were now approaching high school and one day my son said, "Mom, I want a girlfriend and to play on a football team. I don't want to live on the road anymore." This, to me, was a clear message from God speaking to me through my son. It was clearly time to change the trajectory of my life. I decided to settle down and go back to school.

In college I studied social work and worked my way to becoming the executive director of a social service agency that protected children from abuse. During those years I continued to crave academia and achieved a master's degree. I went to Deepak Chopra's wellness college and studied healing and meditation with him, Davidji, and Wayne Dyer. That fire in my belly was heating up again. The energies were swirling and pulling me to learn more. I began to teach at a local university and heard about a professor at Harvard who was teaching positive psychology, called The Science of Happiness. A year later I became post master's certified in positive psychology. I was addicted to this new field of study and applied to be a teacher's assistant. I was accepted and spent another year under the tutelage of the Wholebeing Institute with Dr. Tal Ben Shahar, Maria Sirois, and Megan McDonough. What a dream team to learn from and to practice positive psychology with!

THIRD TRANSFORMATION: *Address my mental and physical health and well-being.*

There is an art and a science to well-being. These studies opened my eyes to things I had been ignoring. As I matured, I stopped thinking about my self-care. My mental and physical health had been neglected. I found myself overweight, depressed, and lethargic. The ugliness of the failed marriages had me believing that nothing really mattered about me personally. I dove completely into a life of motherhood and social services. I liked being invisible to men. In this way, I would no longer be disappointed or betrayed. I enjoyed my career in strengthening others. I was becoming a public speaker, a fundraiser for abuse prevention and family strengthening. I loved being a full-time mother and grandmother.

The energies of yin and yang had simmered to an unrecognizable low. I realized that on a personal level there was only emptiness. On the outside there were productive and successful milestones, on the inside I was numb and cold. There had to be something more, something I was missing. It took courage and self-compassion to look, but I had to take the blinders off, it was time to *see* myself. Transformation to good health and to updating my values map would take me two years of consistent effort. I was beginning to have a direct encounter with *me* and my life.

Along with discovering new priorities, clarification of values, and developing a more positive mindset, I learned to meditate and to practice mindfulness. It is not as easy as it sounds. I had to sort out time to practice, to journal my thoughts, and to connect these practices to daily life in order to experience improved mental and physical health.

A sense of expansive awareness developed. My focus shifted to what mattered and what was important to me. I became more contemplative in prayer and spirituality. Jennifer Haniwald, a teaching assistant with me in the positive psychology program, is also a talented health coach. After one of those all-night long chats while we were at Kripalu, she asked if I would like her to coach me further on my health and wellness journey. I am grateful today that I said "yes." I have lost 60 pounds, I am off the myriad of medicines that I was put on for depression, anxiety, blood pressure, blood sugar, and rheumatoid arthritis. I am happier and healthier.

FOURTH TRANSFORMATION: *I wanted to love my body. This earthen vessel my soul resides in needed attention.*

While at Kripalu studying and teaching positive psychology, I was invited to try a *Let Your Yoga Dance* class with its creator Megha Nancy Buttenhiem. This exercise is based on the philosophy of bringing body, heart, and spiritual health into you through music and movement. It is focused on the seven chakras or energy centers in the body. This was difficult for me at first as the energy centers in my lower extremities were blocked. After the very first full day's efforts, I was filled with joy. I had to learn more and eventually took her course and became an instructor. Now I have spread this same joy throughout the nation, teaching at symposiums, workshops, and yoga studios. It continues to help my body to be flexible and my mind and spirit to be joyful.

I had become comfortable again in my own skin. I changed the inner voice from saying, *You are getting older and can't move like that anymore. Be careful, don't hurt yourself!* to *Move with wild abandon! Let the joy fill your heart! Love your body and be grateful for the beautiful vehicle you are getting through life in.*

FIFTH TRANSFORMATION: *Release the toxic relationships of the past.*

I began feeling empowered on many levels, yet I was still experiencing loneliness. I had accomplished many levels of transformation, yet my true feminine nature still seemed blocked. It was time to accept the challenge...I had to go back there and release the toxic relationships of the past.

My baggage was getting heavy now...shame, codependency, betrayal, and a complete depletion of my feminine energy weighed me down. All I was left with then was anger and bitterness. I had come so far with transformation; now it was time to trust myself enough to recalibrate my heart. I wanted to reveal the most beautiful part of being a woman with someone, sharing intimacy, emotional and physical. I must release the toxins of insecurities, self-doubt, and intense personal feelings of unworthiness. That young girl who felt brave and optimistic started to wake up in me. I became aware and ready to let it all go. It no longer served me to hold onto the baggage. I used the Marie Kondo method of decluttering, not with material things, but with my emotions. I blessed them, blessed the experiences, and untethered them. I guess you just have to be ready to let go, because just like that, they were gone.

SIXTH TRANSFORMATION: *The awakening of Kundalini energy.*

The experience of expanding my sense of self and finding a deeper connection to faith and spirituality had improved my values and, consequently, my behaviors towards myself and others. I was ready to let my *ideal self* step into my life. Kundalini is the energy that suggests that human consciousness, the brain, and the body are all evolving. The three stages of Kundalini are: First, recognizing the need for introspection, getting one's head out of the sand. Second, clarifying values and getting rid of the emotional clutter. Third, awakening to the meaning and true purpose of existence in this time and place. Happily, I had arrived in this place. My energy level has increased and yet I am calm. Pain and challenges have helped me to recognize the need to transform. There is energy and balance in life.

SEVENTH TRANSFORMATION: *The Divine Feminine*

Most of my life was spent searching outside of myself for happiness and peace. It took me across the country and across the ocean. All along the key to those things was inside of me. I was tossed about by misunderstanding, unforgiveness, and bitterness. I relied on a more masculine energy to survive. Now both are in balance. I am a woman filled with divine feminine energy. I can express the higher emotions of love, forgiveness, compassion, sensuality, and gratitude. Being a woman is full of possibilities now. I have never felt so joy-filled, creative, juicy, and wildly free.

About Donna

Donna Martire Miller holds a master's degree in counseling and organizational human resource development. She is a graduate of the Positive Psychology program at Kripalu/Wholebeing Institute, and has studied with Tal Ben Shahar, Megha Nancy Buttenhiem, Deepak Chopra, and Wayne Dyer.

Donna has an adjunct professorship at the University of Bridgeport where she teaches Wellness, Perspectives of Happiness, Practicum/Internship, and other Human Services related courses. Donna developed and held the executive director position for 30 years at HELP FOR KIDS, a positive parenting, family-strengthening center in Southern Connecticut. Donna is owner of "Happily Ever Actions" a business that helps people to live their best life now and that applies cutting-edge research to help people increase happiness and well-being in all areas of life.

"Being a woman is full of possibilities now. I have never felt so joy-filled, creative, juicy, and wildly free."

Donna Martire Miller, MA, CIPP

happilyeveractions.com

Chapter 19

Rise

Lisa Braidwood Ferry

Rise

I let go of doubt and fear

And the sadness that it brings

Sending love and light and gratitude

For all the many things

That lift us up as one

Like laughter, music, loving kindness

With open hearts and open minds

I trust humanity to find this

Spirit of Community for the good of all

For help in this endeavor

Upon Full Moon I call

Smile down upon us gently

Here on Mother Earth

Support us in this trying time

Of destruction and rebirth

Remind us to have faith

And to reflect upon our choices

And like the phoenix we will rise

With peaceful hearts and joyful voices

About Lisa

Lisa Ferry is a certified Usui Reiki and Reiki Sync practitioner. A Bashful Buddha, Lisa is an advocate of the Intuitive Arts and Healing Arts which have been her passion for over 20 years. Study of stones and crystals, aura colors, essential oils, Qi Gong, Oracle card reading, journey work, and intention practice through spell writing has empowered her to dive deep into the world of the spiritual and metaphysical promoting balance within and the healing of mind, body, and soul. It is now Lisa's joy to share her knowledge to help others heal and to be a safe place for conversations about all things intuitive.

"Like the phoenix we will rise with peaceful hearts and joyful voices."

Lisa Braidwood Ferry

thebashfulbuddha@gmail.com

Chapter 20

An Invitation

Elizabeth B. Hill, MSW

When people talk about past lives, I can relate, but not in the way they mean. At 41, I already feel I have lived many lives within this one.

I have moved through loving and leaving. I have lost entire communities of people. I have left religions, divorced, lost babies, loved deeply and been left, loved deeply and chosen to leave. I have hurt people and been hurt. I have learned I was wrong. I have learned I was wronged. I have left homes and built new ones. I have grieved for the loss of many futures I had imagined and many people that I had great visions with and for.

When I hear the word "transformation," rather than one life-altering event, it calls to mind a feeling of an ever-evolving vortex of love, where the world gives me exactly what I need at any given moment.

It may not be what I think I desire or want, but it is all perfectly designed for my transformation, growth, and expansion.

I have discovered that my soul calls in what I desire, whether I understand that invitation or not.

I know there is a purpose in each moment, even those that are terrifying and confusing.

There is a reason I am in each space, in each moment, and with the people I am with. I have learned there are no coincidences.

In fact, there is a reason I am with you, dear reader, right now.

Many of us have navigated on our own for a very long time. It seems the only way, sometimes. It may seem harder to try to get others to carry the weight with us.

This idea of independence also seems to be held up in our society as noble. It is applauded as something to be proud of and impressed by. Yet, rather than providing freedom and nobility, the concept of independence is hoodwinking us. The pressure to be independent keeps people down, where they experience struggle alone.

I invite you to experience a new nobility, which includes being sovereign and getting the support you need to rock-it-out. Queens and CEOs don't do everything (or maybe even anything!) on their own. Queens and CEOs aren't independent.

While transformation takes a lot of reflection and tuning into inner wisdom, navigating a transformation on your own may not serve you.

Sharing your experiences with others may seem very scary at first, but with the right people, I promise it is worth it. Once you experience doing life in a different way - in partnership - you will not go back. There is nothing like co-creating with others who genuinely want what's best for you, who view your wins as their wins, and who you help simply by being you.

I invite you to come play with us in Ladies' Power Lunch. This is what we are up to there.

I invite you to reach out to any of the dear women who are courageous enough to share their stories and inspiration here.

I invite you to let love in. It is time to receive.

Love & Courage,

Elizabeth

About Green Heart Living

Green Heart Living's mission is to make the world a more loving and peaceful place, one person at a time. Green Heart Living Press publishes inspirational books and stories of transformation, making the world a more loving and peaceful place, one book at a time.

Whether you have an idea for an inspirational book and want support through the writing process - or your book is already written and you are looking for a publishing path - Green Heart Living can help you get your book out into the world.

You can meet Green Heart authors on the Green Heart Living YouTube channel and the Green Heart Living podcast.

greenheartliving.com

About Elizabeth B. Hill, MSW

Elizabeth B. Hill is CEO and founder of Green Heart Living. She is the best-selling author and publisher of *The Great Pause: Blessings and Wisdom from COVID-19, Love Notes: Daily Wisdom for the Soul* and *Green Your Heart, Green Your World: Avoid Burnout, Save the World and Love Your Life.*

Elizabeth coaches clients on mindful leadership and writing to heal, inspire, and grow their impact in the world. Trained as a social worker, yoga teacher, and ontological coach, she weaves creativity, spirituality, and mindfulness into her work with clients. With over 15 years of experience writing and leading collaborations in the nonprofit sphere, Elizabeth brings a uniquely engaging approach to collaborative book projects. Elizabeth lives in a matriarchal palace in Connecticut with her family and the neighborhood bears.

Green Heart Living Publications

The Great Pause: Blessings & Wisdom from COVID-19

Love Notes: Daily Wisdom for the Soul

Green Your Heart, Green Your World: Avoid Burnout,
Save the World and Love Your Life

Upcoming Collaborative Projects

Redefining Masculinity

Ladies' Power Lunch Anthology: Success in Any Season

Finding My Marbles

To apply to contribute to an upcoming collaboration,

or to publish an inspirational book of your own, go to

greenheartliving.com

Made in USA - North Chelmsford, MA
1193318_9780999197677
11.12.2020 1621